Saucepans and the Single Girl

Jinx Morgan *and* Judy Perry

WARNER BOOKS

NEW YORK   BOSTON

Warner Books Edition
Copyright © 1965 by Jinx Kragen and Judy Perry
Introduction copyright © 2006 by Jinx Morgan and Judy Perry
All rights reserved.

Warner Books

Time Warner Book Group
1271 Avenue of the Americas, New York, NY 10020
Visit our Web site at www.twbookmark.com.

Printed in the United States of America

First Warner Books Edition: May 2006
10 9 8 7 6 5 4 3 2 1

Library of Congress Cataloging-in-Publication Data
Morgan, Jinx.
Saucepans and the single girl / Jinx Morgan and Judy Perry.—
1st Warner Books ed.
    p.   cm.
Includes index
ISBN-13: 978-0-446-69692-0
ISBN-10: 0-446-69692-7
1. Cookery. I. Perry, Judy. II. Title.
TX715.M8438   2006
641'.5—dc22   2005045672

Cover illustration by Debbie Hanley

Illustrations by Sheila Greenwald

Book design by Stratford Publishing Services, Inc.

To the cadre of single young women who've braved big cities, small apartments, big dreams, and small salaries . . .

And to the men, young and old, who've succumbed to their culinary and winsome wiles. Bless 'em all.

Acknowledgments

A dozen red roses to Leila Porteous, our intrepid editor, who believed that *Saucepans* was as good to go for young women today as it was for the girls of yesterday.

And hats off to Leila's godmother Marian Albee, who first suggested resuscitating the book.

Our special thanks go to Carl Brandt, who has been friend as well as agent for all these years. What can you say about a guy who feeds you scrambled eggs and fine wine during a New York blackout?

Sheila Greenwald's illustrations are as charming as when they appeared in the first incarnation of the book. All the best things are ageless.

A bow to Kallie Shimek, who took our manuscript with its scribbled and scrambled footnotes and pulled it together into a comprehensive whole.

And last, but scarcley least, hugs and kisses to our husbands, Jeff and Jack, who have shared this wonderful journey with us.

Contents

Nouvelle Introduction

Many years past on a sunny summer afternoon, *Saucepans and the Single Girl* was but a chuckle and a whim, sketched out on yellow pads on the beach at Malibu. Just a whim. But that whim wouldn't go away, and before we knew it, we had a book! An honest-to-God hardcover book! We were twenty-four years old.

Fast-forward to 2006. We never dreamed that a new edition would be in demand some forty years later, but we're shamelessly happy to oblige. We've had a great run in the interim and are still taking life in big servings. You get more that way.

Between us, we can lay claim to:

25 houses
Countless dogs and cats of various generic brands
3,267 successful dinner parties
19 just okay dinner parties (blame it on the guests)
2 downright disasters
0 kitchen fires
3 husbands (not simultaneously)
2 perfect children, 3 fabulous stepchildren, and 11 grandchildren (world-class adorable)
Millions of travel miles, not all first-class

12 hurricanes and 7 earthquakes
1 Caribbean hotel

Here's what wasn't on the scene when we wrote the book:

Cuisinarts
Bread machines
Fusion food
Panini makers
Beefalo
Espresso machines
Microwaves
The Food Network
Botox
Wonderbras
Casual Fridays
Casual sex
. . . and hooking up was just something you did with a rain-
    bow trout.

Here's what single girls have now that we didn't:

iPods
Cosmopolitans
Spell-checkers
Double lattes
Choo's shoes
Spandex

Personal trainers
BlackBerrys
. . . and, best of all, the Wonderful World of Takeout.

We blush at the thought of a few things we endorsed in *Saucepans:*

Canned everything—from white sauce to wild rice
Dried everything—from chives to parsley
Instant potatoes, tea, coffee—you name it
Meat tenderizer
Cooking wine (well, we *were* on the cheap back then)

So, forgive us our trespasses. Throughout the new *Saucepans,* we'll redeem our past and recommend how to use the real thing instead of those pantry pretenders by using these road signs:

🕐 Historical update

♪ Pantry/kitchen update

💡 Even better!

❓ What were we thinking?

But if you're miles from your closest fresh-food emporium, your Manolos are killing you, and you've impulsively issued some kind of dinner invitation, go ahead. Fall back on dried, instant, canned. We'll close ranks; count on it.

What's still amazingly seductive:

An elegant meal prepared at home by you, for you and someone whose socks you'd like to knock off.

So! Life is like a sumptuous feast: beautiful to behold, plenty
for everyone, and second helpings are even better. Enjoy the
banquet as much as we've relished ours and never stop planning
the next one. Godspeed!

Jinx Morgan
Judy Perry

Introduction

OR:

Why We Bothered

Three years ago we packed away the proverbial sheepskins and our Chaucer translations and left the ivied halls to become independent and salaried. Since we had managed to maintain our friendship as roommates in college, we had high hopes that the arrangement would prosper off campus as well.

We succeeded in finding jobs, although our dreams of wearing hats to the office faded as we each learned that degrees in English qualify one for a limited realm of responsibility in the business world—usually confined either to preparing the coffee for the office staff or watering the rubber plant.

We also managed to find an apartment, although it, too, fell somewhere short of our ambitions. While it did not have white wall-to-wall carpeting, a sunken Roman bathtub, or even an antique French phone, neither did it have rats, cockroaches, or faulty plumbing. In this life, one learns to grasp at even these small blessings.

Our gay young life all but died aborning. Everything was blissful until we discovered that for all his talent, old Geoffrey Chaucer couldn't help us much when it came to running a domicile art-fully with a modicum of money and knowledge. Pride we had; proficiency we had not.

TV dinners or hearty bowls of soup were enough to fill our inner needs, but entertaining caused us many a migraine. We had had visions of divine BBD&O men and intimate little dinners complete with candlelight and wine, but it wasn't long before we realized that it would take more than a fallen soufflé or a sticky fondue to give us the bravado one needs to entertain with ease and rakish glamour.

Things have improved since the days when a boiled egg was too formidable to contemplate, and now we can face a dinner party or a recipe for pâté without blanching. As a result, we feel duty-bound to pass our shoddy little secrets along to other girls who have been pitched unceremoniously into the world of pay-checks and pot holders. However, when two rank amateurs invade the exalted realm of haute cuisine, a word of explanation is in order.

This book began to take shape on a warm California day as we sat slothfully reminiscing about those days of near-starvation we survived as fledgling career girls. It occurred to us that there had been cookbooks written for people who love to cook, people who hate to cook, bachelors, gourmets, wolves, and just about everyone but the poor working girl. And so, after begging our friends for all of their battle-scarred recipes and rummaging through our own meager files, we began.

Surrounded by oceans of 3 × 5 cards, we sat down to fill in the one gap still existing on the shelves of cookbook literature. Bearing in mind that most career girls are on strict monthly budgets ($200 for clothes, $20 for taxis, $30 for hairdresser, $50 for rent, $10 for food),⊕ we have tried to keep our recipes and menus realistically geared to this type of financial chicanery.

We can't boast gleaming test kitchens with shining aluminum sinks and flameless cooking as do those wonderfully capable and starchy ladies who edit your big fat cookbooks. More often than not, one of us was drying her hair in the oven or our elephantine dog was shuffling about chewing up chapters as fast as we could reel them out. You'll notice, in the chapters we managed to rescue, that we have developed a secret code that is the envy of the CIA. But once the code has been broken, it's really quite simple: a recipe marked * can be found in the index, and a recipe marked † can be refrigerated at that point for later warming.

With the mechanics out of the way, what else can we say except that we've been through it too? We know these recipes work, for we survived. And so can you.

⊕ You can tailor your fiscal apportioning by randomly sprinkling extra zeros here and there as needed.

1

Left-Handed Gourmet

OR:

Your Right Arm

It's easy enough to delude a male Saturday dinner guest into believing that he has discovered a real jewel of a gourmet, but what about that inevitable night when old Charlie, who fixes your flat tires, repairs your sink, lends you money, and occasionally is caught giving you an adoring glance, buys you a drink after work, God bless him, and you forgetfully invite him up for an intimate little dinner? Hmmmm.

Now if you have been flat-footed and budget-minded, you have nothing but that dreary pound of ground round that you put out this morning, and your larder boasts a dandy box of instant rice and some dehydrated potatoes. This is fine for an evening of soul-searching with Dr. Kildare,⊕ but you just can't do it to Charlie.

Your pantry will be a godsend at a time like this when you're hearing the death knell of your reputation as a cook. You'll feel a lot better about the fifty cents you spent on marinated artichoke hearts last week. Our first apartment didn't afford us the luxury of a pantry, and we were forced to keep our goodies in old Macy's boxes under the beds. It was a bit embarrassing if we forgot to get them out before our guests arrived, for we felt slightly silly saying, "Excuse me, I'm just getting the wild rice," as we groped around under the bed. To this day, we have friends who swear that we had our own paddy under there. But no matter where you stash them, you'll need these items at least for emergency

---

⊕ This is too hard to explain. Just think George Clooney in scrubs. Sigh.

purposes; so find a good hiding place, and keep it a secret that wild mastodons couldn't drag out of you.

If you're half as innocent as we were when we left those ivied halls for the Big Life, you'll need the following lists to start your shopping. If, after reading them, you're feeling very smug because, of course, you didn't need someone to tell you all those silly old things, then forget it. This book is for domestic fledglings who are either not afraid to admit it or just plain can't hide it.

The following dull little items are just that, but we'll bet you won't be able to live without them.

Baking Powder
Baking Soda
Bouillon Cubes (Chicken and Beef)
Coffee (Instant and Ground)
Cornstarch
Cracked Black Pepper (There *is* a difference)
Dried Milk Concentrate
Dry Mustard
Egg Noodles
Flour
Garlic
Garlic Powder
Instant♪ Minced Onion

♪ Instant espresso isn't bad, but other instant pantry items are poor seconds. Go for the real thing.

Instant Potatoes
Ketchup
Lemon Juice (Bottled)♪
Macaroni
Meat Tenderizer♪♪
Mustard
Onions
Pepper
Plain Gelatin
Potatoes
Precooked Instant Rice
Salad Dressing (Dehydrated)
Salad Oil♪♪♪
Salt
Shortening
Soups (You'll use gallons of cream of mushroom, possibly onion)
Spaghetti
Sugar (Granulated White, Brown, and Powdered)
Tabasco Sauce

♪ We'd love to know that you'll eschew bottled and frozen juices; freshly squeezed juices are readily available today. And how hard is it to squeeze a lemon?

♪♪ This is no longer gastronomically correct. The only substitute is an acid-based marinade—or you can ante up for more tender cuts.

♪♪♪ Salad Oil

Salad oil is really sort of a generic term. Actually, there are two kinds of oil that should interest you. Use canola oil for times when you don't want the richness and flavor of olive oil. Don't know when that might be? A salad dressing is excellent with olive oil, unless it's Asian in nature. Then we'd use peanut oil and rice wine vinegar. Sauté meats in olive oil. Keep them both on hand and buy in small amounts; oil can turn rancid. Eeeuw.

Tea Bags
Vanilla
Wine Vinegar
Worcestershire Sauce

One last pantry update. Check out the Asian section of your supermarket. Experiment with hoisin, plum sauce, fish sauce, chili paste, sesame oil, and black bean sauce. These are great to smear on chicken, ribs, and fish and will add to a killer salad dressing.

The most mundane cook uses herbs and spices, even if it be only paprika; but if you're going to feign the role of a gourmet, your reputation will increase in proportion to the number of mysterious jars and cans on your shelf. We have a friend whose shaker-topped spices have long since plugged up (the nasty little things have a way of doing that), yet she still wields those bottles with furor—says it fools her guest and makes *her* feel better.

Use them lavishly and experimentally. The list may seem long when you consider that there are only two days out of the week that you'll be taking the time to whip up Chicken Cacciatore or a tempting Herbed Roast Leg of Lamb, but remember that even you and your roommate are going to get awfully bored with string beans melted down every night, and you never know what you can pitch in the pot with them if you have plenty of herbs. It's a good idea to buy them in airtight containers, as they dry up easily.

Basil𝄑	Dill Weed	Onion Salt
Bay Leaves	Ginger	Oregano
Beau Monde	Marjoram	Paprika
Cayenne Pepper	Minced Parsley	Rosemary
Chili Powder	Flakes	Tarragon
Cinnamon	MSG𝄑𝄑	Thyme
Curry Powder	Nutmeg	

𝄑𝄑 Well, here's a red flag. Once upon a time, this additive was accepted in the most sophisticated of cooking circles. Today, skip it!

♪ Herbs

Here's a subject we want to deal with and be over it. Most often, fresh herbs are a bright note in your dish, one that dried herbs can't attain. But! You'll soon learn which ones are stellar in their virgin, fresh state and which ones can stand being dried and confined to a little glass prison. Ones we think are quite okay in jars (try www.penzeys.com, a fantastic source):

Assorted Chile Powders:	Italian Herb Seasoning
Ancho, Chipotle, Adobo	Oregano
Cumin	Tarragon
Garlic Salt	Thyme
Herbes de Provence	

Be sure to keep them in the dark—literally. They'll keep longer away from light and heat.

Ones that aren't as pungent when dried and therefore not as effective (most supermarkets now carry fresh herbs, but if you have a green thumb, try growing your own on a windowsill):

Basil	Rosemary
Dill	Sage

Just remember that there's an important exchange rate when swapping fresh for dried. You'll need to use two to three times the amount of dried when substituting with fresh.

You're going to have to break down and buy the following staples for your refrigerator, but best to buy in niggling little amounts for weekday needs, as they spoil. Since they're not wickedly high in calories *or* imagination, we hate to waste money on them.

Bacon   Eggs
Bread   Green Onions
Butter   Lettuce
Cheeses (Gourmet   Milk
    departments offer   Tomatoes
    wheels of delightfully
    stinky cheeses that
    will supplement the
    usual cheddar and
    provolone or
    Monterey Jack)

Obviously, if you have inherited the usual apartment refrigerator with a freezer that would give a single drumstick claustrophobia, you'll have to forgo most of the following. Whatever you do, don't give up ice cubes; you need them after a long day over a hot typewriter.⊕

⊕ The precursor to your PC. If you're curious, one can probably be viewed at the Smithsonian.

French Bread (Cut in
serving size and *then*
freeze)
Frozen*ᵈ* Chives

Frozen Fruits
Frozen Juices
Frozen Vegetables
Meats

The next list is one from which you can pick and choose as
you will, and it's by far the most fun. The greatest part of it is that
these are the blessed items that always saved us on those dreadful
evenings when old Charlie was just standing there shuffling and
waiting for a repeat on those Rock Cornish game hens.

Artichoke Hearts (Both Marinated and Plain Canned or
Frozen)
Bread Crumbs
Canned*ᵈᵈ* Crabmeat
Canned Hollandaise Sauce
Canned Medium Shrimp
Canned Mushrooms
Canned Sardines

ᵈ Those frozen assets are not always assets. Frequent the fresh-
produce section instead.

ᵈᵈ We don't know any other way to buy sardines but in cans, but those
other canned things aren't necessary substitutes in today's world.
As we move through *Saucepans*, we'll give you options and recipes.

Canned White Sauce*ƒ*
Canned Wild Rice (Never, never attempt the start-from-scratch kind—you're doomed if you do)*ƒƒ*
Chutney (a horrendous expense, but well worth it)*ƒƒƒ*
Cooking Wine (Sherry, Burgundy, and a Dry White)
Croutons
Garlic Spread (Prepared)
Grated Parmesan Cheese
Grated Romano Cheese (Good in salads)

ƒ White Sauce

Okay. We're going to deal with this right up front and admit our embarrassment at this suggestion. *Never* buy canned cream sauce. Below we've given you the easiest answer, adapted from the esteemed Ms. Child:

Cream Sauce

Melt 2½ tablespoons butter in a heavy-bottomed saucepan. Blend in 3½ tablespoons flour to make a smooth paste. Stir over medium heat until it foams for a couple of minutes. It should be a (what else?) buttery yellow. Remove from heat. When the bubbling stops, add 1½ cups hot milk, whisking

---

ƒƒ See note on page 86.
ƒƒƒ There must have been a chutney embargo back then? At any rate, it's affordable now.

with fervor until blended. Now whisk more slowly, getting into all the areas of the saucepan. Slowly dribble in up to another ½ cup hot milk to desired consistency. Should coat the spoon nicely. To keep skin from forming, press a sheet of plastic wrap directly on the sauce. Will keep for 3 days. Reheat very gently.

Now, if you're in a pinch, Contadina, Buitoni, and other reliable producers of Italian food package an Alfredo sauce (both light and not so light) that is just fine. You'll want to thin it down a bit with some chicken broth, maybe add a little thyme or whatever complements your dish, but trust us. It works. It's only cream sauce—béchamel in Julia Child's world, *mon enfant*—with a bit of Parmesan added. Consider it seriously. Just hide that plastic container in the trash compactor. That's something else we didn't have in 1965!

Horseradish
Instant Espresso
Olive Oil
Slivered Almonds
Smoked Oysters
Smoked Salmon (Good luck trying to find it)𝛿
Soy Sauce

𝛿 You won't need a good luck charm—it's everywhere now.

Honest-to-Goodness Tea Leaves
Tomato Paste
Tomato Sauce
Tuna (Of course)

An awesome list and even more frightening to pay for if you attempt to bring in the above harvest all at one time. Try buying only one or two of the exciting items when you're picking up ground round and peanut butter. If you amortize the expense this way, you may even succeed in fooling yourself.

SPIRITED DISCUSSION

Never, never neglect to have a budget-busting bottle of Mumm's on hand for celebrating raises and broken engagements (whew!), and don't forget that a meal is only a meal without wine.

And so here we are at that grim little subject that we kept hoping would go away. Nevertheless, our frail knowledge of wines will get you through an evening quite passably. From there on, you're on your own. Should the subject hook you, there are several kindly gentlemen⊕ who have thoughtfully written entertaining and learned theses on it.

⊕ And ladies, too.

Before you ever approach the problems of nomenclature and nonsense, remember the first simple rules and you'll always be safe:

1. If you're not sure of the wine, it's a good idea to serve red wine with red meat and white with white meat. In general, red is good with steaks, chops, roasts, cheese dishes, and Italian food. Less expensive red wine is good for marinating cheap cuts of meat and for adding to stews or other meat-vegetable casseroles. White wine complements more delicately flavored foods— seafood, poultry, omelets, and even scrambled eggs. Should you feel adventurous, there's no harm in mixing your wines and meats. It's an old rule that need not be observed rigidly.

2. Red wines, especially the heavy, full ones, should be served at room temperature. This does not mean leaving them on the fire escape in the midst of a New York summer. Most white wines are best when thoroughly chilled; rosé should also be chilled.

3. Remember that dry or medium-bodied wines are best served with main dishes; save the sweet wines for desserts or fruits.

4. A tulip-shaped glass is an adequate and acceptable means of serving almost all wines—even Champagne, according to many experts.

5. Try to buy your wine from a liquor store that has an extensive wine cellar. The owner or manager will most likely be more

qualified to give you accurate advice on which wines are dry or sweet, tart or soft, etc. Don't be afraid to ask questions—it's flattering.

6. All wines should be stored horizontally. This allows the sediment to settle and prevents the cork from drying out. The cork, incidentally, should be about two inches long.

7. Wine snobs suggest—and wisely so—opening the bottle an hour or so before the meal to allow the wine to "breathe." If you'll put the bottle in a basket carrier then, the sediment will settle again by mealtime. *Don't* wave the bottle around like a baton as you bring it to the table.

8. On all bottles of imported wines, look for the words *Appellation Contrôlée*—your assurance that the contents have been required to meet certain standards. The name of a good wine merchant or shipper on the bottle is an added bit of insurance.

THE WINES OF FRANCE

Bordeaux

The Bordeaux country produces both red and white wines; the red wines are clarets. If you're buying a bottle of Bordeaux, be sure to look for the words *Mis en Bouteilles au Château*. Our Berlitz dictionary tells us that that means it was bottled at the château where the grapes were grown—another bit of insurance. Also look for the name of the château on the cork itself. Within Bordeaux, there are many areas that produce good and great wine, but we'll touch upon some of the most well known.

MÉDOC
- are full-bodied and dignified
- produces both red and white wines, but the clarets are the best
- a few of the great wines of the Médoc that *you* can't afford but might make a worthy gift are Château-Latour, Château-Lafite, Château Margaux, Haut-Brion (Graves), and Mouton-Rothschild

GRAVES
- produces lots of red, some white wines
- the dry whites are some of the best anywhere
- are not as full-bodied as those of the Médoc, but are very fine

ST. EMILION AND POMEROL
- more robust and fruity than those of the Médoc; hearty
- two great growths that would be good gifts if you've just had a raise are Château Cheval Blanc and Château Ausone
- excellent with rich game or heavy red meats

Barsac
- a very sweet white Bordeaux

Sauternes
- some of the best sweet white wines in the world
- they are to be sipped—and then only with desserts and fruits, please!
- one great label: Château d'Yquem
- there are some dry Sauternes, but if you're an aficionado of really dry wines, better steer clear

Burgundy

Burgundy wines, both red and white, are rich and full. When they're good, they can't be surpassed and are often called the King of Wines. Burgundy country is divided quite simply into two main sections: the Côte de Nuits, where great red wines are produced from the Pinot Noir grapes, and the Côte de Beaune, where the Chardonnay and Pinot Blanc grapes are grown to create the great white wines.

White Burgundy
- is considered to have white Bordeaux beaten by a mile
- Pouilly-Fuissé is an excellent white wine from the Mâconnais section of Burgundy
- Chablis is a clean and very dry white Burgundy
- the fruity white wines of Meursault and Montrachet are truly delightful

Red Burgundy
- Beaujolais is a light, fruity red Burgundy
- best growths of heavy red Burgundy include Vosne-Romanée, Corton, and Chambolle Musigny
- the Chambertin area produces some truly great red wines

Champagne

Champagne—is any wine more festive or heady? (If you don't believe us, ask your own head the next morning.) Its great virtue lies in that it may be served at any time and with any food.

- look for three words on the bottle: Brut (very dry), Sec (semidry), or Doux (sweet)
- in buying by label, it's best to trust the shipper's name. There are no vineyard names, as the grapes are blended from different vineyards to achieve the best bouquet. Reliable shippers include Heidsieck, Krug, Perrier-Jouet, and Mumm
- the names Epernay and Reims on a bottle of Champagne designate locale and type of grape (white and black, respectively). Some wine authorities contend that the best Champagne comes from the Reims area

Rhône

While the Rhône doesn't produce a number of great wines, it does boast several real jewels:

- Châteauneuf-du-Pape, a dry, light red that is a true delight and even goes well with white meats and cheeses

- rosé from the Tavel area is some of the best in the world
- Château Grillet is included in the best white wines, full and heady
- Côte Rôtie, akin to Beaujolais
- Hermitage

Loire

The Loire Valley is best known for its Anjou—a light, fruity rosé wine. Others include:

- Muscadet, a light, fairly dry white wine
- Sancerre, a dry, less fruity wine
- Pouilly-Fumé, a dry white

Provence

Very few Provence wines are exported, but should you be able to get your hands on some, look out! They are pleasant and light, but very heady.

Alsace

Alsatian wines—clean, spicy, fresh—are directly related to German wines in that they are a product of the same grapes. They are the only French wines known by grape rather than vineyard or shipper. Three grapes whose names you might look for:

- Sylvaner, which produces light, fresh wines
- Traminer, which is more refined and sweet
- Riesling, noble and dignified white wines

THE WINES OF GERMANY

German wines vary from light and dry to rich and sweet, but you'll find that the white wines are the best. Almost all are grown from Sylvaner, Riesling, and Traminer grapes.

MOSELLE
- are the lightest, driest German wines
- an added trick: it always comes in a green bottle
- one of the best is Bernkasteler Doktor
- these are gay, sprightly wines for happy occasions

RHINE
- full-bodied, fruity
- include wines from Rheingau, Rheinhessen, and Rheinpfalz
- always come in brown bottles
- stately, dignified wines in comparison to the Moselles

THE WINES OF CALIFORNIA

A counterpart of every European wine can be found in California wines. The finest come from Napa, Sonoma, Santa Cruz, and the Santa Clara Valley—our old stomping grounds, as the expression goes. California wines are rapidly achieving acclaim, and rightly so, for the constant climate ensures reliability. To classify just the dinner wines simply:

White

SAUTERNES
Semillon—can be dry or sweet
Sauvignon Blanc—dry

RHINE
Sylvaner—spicy, fresh
Riesling—full-bodied

CHABLIS
Pinot Blanc—full, clean, very dry
Chardonnay—very dry, full

Red

BURGUNDY
Pinot Noir—full-bodied, heavy, and dry

CLARET
Cabernet—driest of the clarets
Zinfandel—fruity and dry

VINO—tart, dry

ROSÉ—light, pink, fruity; often sweet

Excellent California vineyards include, among a great many others, Louis Martini, Paul Masson, Almadén, and Inglenook Farms.♥

VINTAGES☉

The following list of vintage years will guarantee your safety in selecting your wines. Of course, you won't have any money left over, either, as vintage years are often dear. But that's your problem; you can always stick to the little old Grape-Stomper if you want to be that way about it. . . .

RED BORDEAUX
Great: 1961, 1959, 1953
Good: 1962, 1958, 1955

♥ Should you want to amp up your California vineyard selections, try Château St. Jean, Edna Valley, Rombauer, Hess Select, Wild Horse, Sterling, and Duckhorn. Newer world entries are Chilean reds, Australian reds, Oregon Pinot Noirs, and New Zealand Sauvignon Blancs. Many South African wines are making big noise, and even Texas is getting into the act with wines from its hill country.

☉ Ah, vintages. This would be a good time to suggest that you invest in a wine-buying guide dating from, say, 2000 to the present. The one we use is well indexed and would fit right next to your cell phone in the depths of your Birkin bag.

WHITE BORDEAUX
Great: 1962, 1961
Good: 1959 (Sauternes only)

RED BURGUNDY
Great: 1962, 1961, 1959
Good: 1957, 1953

WHITE BURGUNDY[1]
Great: 1962, 1961
Good: 1963, 1960, 1958, 1957

BEAUJOLAIS[1]
Great: 1961
Good: 1962

RHÔNE
Great: 1961 (red only), 1955, 1952
Good: 1962, 1958, 1957

LOIRE
Good: 1962, 1961

ALSACE
Good: 1962, 1961, 1959

---

[1]Improve little with age.

CHAMPAGNE
Great: 1962, 1961, 1952
Good: 1959, 1957, 1955, 1953

RHINE
Great: 1959
Good: 1962, 1961, 1958

MOSELLE
Great: 1959
Good: 1962, 1961, 1958

CALIFORNIA
Variance is negligible

As for your liquor cabinet, it's a good idea to have a small bottle (pint) of each of the following five liquors if you can eke it out of the rent money somehow. You might let the man of the hour's taste dictate when it comes to the purchase of anything as staggering as a fifth or a quart of any one kind.

Bourbon
Brandy
Gin
Scotch
Vermouth (Dry)
Vodka

Tonic
Soda Water
Cocktail Onions
Green Cocktail Olives
Various Mixes

Basic Highball: Put several ice cubes in an eight- to ten-ounce glass. Pour two ounces liquor over ice, and fill to top with water, soda, or whatever mix you like.

Martini: Put several ice cubes in a small pitcher. Pour in five parts gin to one part dry vermouth over the ice. Aficionados tell us that you should stir no more than twenty times—seems it "bruises" the gin. Strain the martini into a glass and plop in an olive. If you've made up a big batch, remove the ice cubes and store the pitcher in the refrigerator. A Gibson is nothing but a martini with an onion instead of an olive.

If you're blighted with helpful guests who always want something like an Acapulco Smile or a White Whale, you'd better invest in a good bartender's guide or else strike them off your list forevermore.

HELPERS
OR: WHY DIDN'T YOU
THINK OF THAT?

1. By all means, invest in one of the fattest cookbooks you can find—not Escoffier,☺ but one of the type the national magazines put out. They're written for even the most cautious and

---

☺ France's predecessor to our own Julia Child, Jacques Pepin, or Wolfgang Puck.

will tell you everything basic that you need to know, from boiling eggs to scraping burned toast. ℓ

2. Cut packages of frozen vegetables in half; each half is just right for two medium servings, and you won't have three or four teaspoons of creamed corn hanging around weeks later.

3. If you cut a loaf of French bread into serving slices before you freeze it, you can take out just what you need *when* you need it instead of waiting for a big occasion to justify a whole loaf.

4. Buy eggs by the half dozen; if you wink at the callow youth that mans the check-stand, he'll willingly cut the box in half for you.

5. Shop on weeknights—don't waste a Saturday when the stores are twice as busy.

6. Buy dairy products in the smallest cartons available.

7. Any casserole can be made ahead of time—like the night before—which is a boon for entertaining or for just you and your roommate. Be sure to cook it for the whole time except for the last fifteen minutes or so. When you come home, pop it in the oven and heat until bubbling.

ℓ Of all the gazillions of cookbooks available today, we still turn to *The Joy of Cooking* or *Mastering the Art of French Cooking* when we need accurate information or want to be inspired.

8. Gargantuan salads are easy for you to make on a weeknight, and they make great substitutes for vegetables. The Classic Oil and Vinegar Dressing consists of three parts oil (preferably olive) to one part wine vinegar or lemon juice. If you're a purist, you'll press some garlic into it along with dry mustard, cracked black pepper, salt, and perhaps some basil or dill. If you're lazy, you'll settle for garlic powder, salt, and pepper. A word, please: always use less dressing than you think you'll need. Toss. Then add more if you see fit. Nothing is worse than too much dressing slogging around the bottom of the salad bowl.

9. Don't be too cheap. Try to eat steaks and chops as often as you feel is financially feasible during the week.*♪* Save the gooey little Stroganoff for weekends when you can share it—and the laurels. A steak or a hearty casserole is no more expensive and a lot better for you, but we'll save those lectures, for we know only too well that your dear old mother back in Hoboken will write them to you weekly anyway.

10. In lieu of a double boiler, a smaller saucepan inside a large one will do just fine . . . looks very inefficient, but who cares?

11. When you're entertaining, be sure to give your meal a good mental shakedown for texture, taste, eye appeal, and availability of serving dishes. Prepare a menu to be tacked up some-

---

♪ These days we're more likely to choose chicken breasts, pasta, or salads for weekday meals.

where in the kitchen a week ahead of time. If you stare at it long enough, you'll become old friends, and you may think of some more tasks you can do ahead of time. We once forgot a tasty little liver pâté that we had spent an entire Thursday evening making. We didn't find it until we staggered out on Sunday morning with a creditable hangover.

12. Make extra ice cubes and keep them in a plastic bag in the freezer. This saves running upstairs to borrow them—though you never know whom you'll meet that way. . . .

13. Never, never forget to put your meat out in the morning to defrost.*ƒ* Otherwise, you'll kick yourself all the way to the deli. We found an even better way than letting it make a mess all over the counter. Take the meat out the night before and leave it out overnight. Return it to the refrigerator while you're scrambling the eggs (your mother will write to you about Good Breakfasts, too). It will be completely defrosted without drooling and running the risk of spoiling in hot weather.

14. Same thing with orange juice*ƒƒ*—make it at night. Nothing is more maddening than chasing that hard little core around the pitcher when you've already overslept.

ƒ We've learned that it's more prudent to put frozen meat in the refrigerator the night before and let it thaw slowly and at a nice arctic temperature.

ƒƒ See note on page 8.

15. Use instant minced onion*ℓ* instead of chopping and weeping. Saves on mascara.

16. When cleanup time rolls around, as it inevitably does, why not fly in the face of convention and start with those gummy pots and pans? You won't be so tempted to leave them soaking for two weeks, and you can always lay in a fresh supply of soap-suds for the glasses and silver.

17. If you're fatties like we were—or inclined to be, anyway—skip desserts. You'll save money and feel wonderfully virtuous.

18. There's a marvelous invention on the market, and it's made specifically for apartment dwellers or picnic pros. A tiny little barbecue*ℓℓ* resembling a giant paper cup, this grill uses only six rolled-up newspapers for broiling, and the flavor is definitely one of charcoal-broiled foods. Use it on your balcony or take it along on your next outing.

19. Learn to make a good cup of coffee. There are two kinds of coffeepots: percolators (where the water goes up) and drip (where the water goes down). Electric percolators are great; the

---

ℓ See note on page 7.

ℓℓ We haven't seen one of these in decades, but there are any number of apartment-friendly grills out there today. Later, we'll talk about ridged stove-top grill pans that will keep you off the balcony on a nippy night.

drip variety also makes good coffee. We never could make non-electric percolators work—they have a sneaky way of boiling over when you're not looking. Now you've got your pot. Keep it reasonably clean, though there's no need to scrub it each time. The secret to good coffee lies in accurate measurement. The water should just hit the level indicated by the manufacturer; if you peer inside, you can see those little lines. The coffee (regular grind for percolators and drip grind for drip pots) should be ladled with a coffee measure from the dime store☺ instead of an old tablespoon.

POTS AND PANS

Undoubtedly, you have in your family tree an assortment of relatives who have long since forgotten that you had your sixth birthday something over fifteen years ago. Consequently, the doting souls continue to send Little Miss Cosmetics and Frenchy the Whale Bubble Bath every year at Christmas. If you're intelligent, you'll mimeograph☺☺ the following list of life's essentials and casually tuck it in Great-Aunt Minnie's Christmas card this year. She'll be glad to send you something useful, and she'll

---

☺ Yes, indeed, there once was something called a dime store, though truth be told, there wasn't much in it for a dime even back then.

☺☺ Mimeographs, and the mess they made of our manicures, have gone the way of the dial telephone. Just use your handy copy machine.

probably be snowed by your sudden interest in the homey arts. Better send it early before she lays in that supply of Little Miss Toilet Water.

Small Saucepan (1 quart)
Medium Saucepan
   (2 quarts)
Large Saucepan (3 quarts)
Big Kettle (10 quarts—
   for cooking noodles, etc.)
10-inch French Chef Skillet
   with Cover
Colander

Assorted Casserole Dishes
Coffeepot (Preferably electric)
Assorted Baking Dishes
Pie Tin or Glass Pie Pan
Pot Holders and Aprons
Plastic Refrigerator Storage
   Containers

If you should make a clean sweep this year, next year you can run off this list and you'll really be set:

Electric Frying Pan
Electric Blender
Double Boiler
Electric Toaster
Chafing Dish

Dutch Oven
Cookie Sheets
Muffin Tins
Ramekins or Individual
   Casseroles

So next year it's back to Little Miss Cosmetics. Ho-hum. On to greener fields.

Tools You'll Never Trade

Life after Williams-Sonoma has rendered us ever more effi-
cient and creative, with a battery of gadgets at our disposal.
The culinary world is rife with these new and useful tools, so
get out your Christmas list again. Some aren't so new; it's just
that we forgot to mention them forty years ago.

Rabbit corkscrew—first things first, after all
5-quart heavy Dutch oven—think Le Creuset or Lodge
8-quart heavy pot—Le Creuset or Lodge again
Stove-top ridged grill pan, preferably shallow—you use it
    just as you would a barbecue. Muddle around online
    until you find one you like. We like Anolon's 12-inch
    shallow round with a heatproof handle.
Pasta pot with strainer/steamer baskets
Mixing bowls with rubber bottoms
Best knives you can afford: Henckels, Wusthof, Global. You
    can get by with an 8- to 10-inch chef's knife, a paring
    knife, and a serrated bread/tomato knife.
Microwave
KitchenAid mixer with attachments—this is called com-
    mitment
Food processor with a few of the fancy blades (shredder, slicer)
Mini food processor for the small stuff—shallots, herbs
Spring-loaded chef's tongs—indispensable

Panini sandwich press—guys love the oozing, crispy sandwiches they can build.

Alligator vegetable dicer (Williams-Sonoma online catalog)—chops half an onion in perfect dice in a way that a food processor just can't muster.

Aerator for your morning latte—no need to stand in line at Starbucks (though you never know whom you'll meet . . .)

Instant-read meat thermometer (look for Taylor brand)

Rasp/zester—a long, raggedy, metal spatula-like grater on a handle. Great for zesting citrus and for grating a bit of Parmesan for your penne.

Ball whisk—this looks like your fairy godmother's magic wand with little round silicone balls at the end of 9–13 wires. Quite edgy.

Garlic press and garlic peeler—the latter is a strange little rubber tube, most inexpensive, that works like a charm. Nestle the garlic clove inside, roll it back and forth on the counter, and it sheds its skin like an embarrassed snake.

Online shopping brings all of these to your home via www.williams-sonoma.com or www.chefscatalog.com. Or Google your way through the land of one thousand clicks until you find the treasure you're seeking.

2
How to Make a Silk Purse
Out of an Et Cetera

There are two distinct attitudes about poverty. One is hang-dog embarrassment. This is not for us. The other is a rakish devil-may-care pose, which we highly recommend. Let's face it—until working girls get a stronger lobby in Washington,⊕ you're going to be stuck with that meager wage, so you might as well learn to live with it.

Since there are so many goodies on which to spend your weekly stipend, we doubt that you will haunt the housewares departments blowing your pay on a matched set of Limoges. Enough time for that later. On the other hand, you can't serve a beautiful meal from a shoe box and expect to create little eddies of elegance.

Fear not—there *are* artistic and even elegant ways to decorate and serve your meals that won't necessitate hocking the family jewels.

Where to serve dinner is the first problem of apartment dwellers. The answer is anywhere. Assuming that you don't have a dining room, the living room is usually more spacious and gracious than any other room in the apartment. And don't forget the kitchen—it's warm and cozy, and your stove makes a great buffet table, for everything stays hot! We once went to a spaghetti dinner that was served right from stove to plate, and it was a smashing success.

⊕ It's been a long, hard slog, but we're getting there. In the meantime, here's some supplemental reading we wish had been around back in our day: *Nice Girls Don't Get Rich*, by Lois P. Frankel, PhD.

If you have a coffee table, you must have discovered by now that it also makes a perfectly adequate dining table when surrounded by a bright galaxy of floor cushions. Another good solution is the enlistment of those ever-popular TV trays. But it's worth your time to shop around for a handsome set. We know, for we were the less-than-proud owners of a really tacky set that came complete with orange-painted flamingos. However, a can of paint and a firm resolve never to use them without beautiful mats took care of everything. Card tables, the old standby of buffet-givers, are also serviceable and convenient.

And here's one you might not have thought of. If your apartment is *really* basic, why not cover your ironing board with a bright cloth and use that for your buffet table? It certainly won't make owners of Chippendale envious, but it does show a certain brave ingenuity.

After you have decided what kind of table you're going to use, you will run smack bang into another soul-shattering problem: how are you going to serve Flaming Beef Burgundy on those red plastic dishes that you grabbed so greedily before your mother could give them to the junkman? Now comes the time when you absolutely have to spend a few pennies; there is just no way of getting around it. However, don't lose your head—you'll find that many variety and department stores carry a selection of handsome china for very little money. And, if you're a big-city dweller, you'll find that hotel supply stores sell china, glassware, and silver for about one-third of their retail price. No matter where you buy them, don't think of your china and glassware as being your lifelong choice. Try to select something that will be chic and serviceable now, but that you won't regret tossing out with your old fraternity pins and pressed corsages when wedding bells peal.

For instance, we chose a stark white china, which was marvelous because it went with all our mats and napkins and honestly looked different each time we served a meal on it. Another idea might be a rough brown pottery, which looks cozy with checked napkins and mats but can be very sophisticated when coupled with white linen and fragile wineglasses. Look around and see what strikes your fancy. One caution, however: when you are limited to a small number of dishes, you'll find that you will have much greater opportunity for variety in your table settings if the dishes you select are plain ones.

When it comes to glasses, don't waste money on expensive ones—your inebriated guests will break them twice as quickly as early Woolworth stemware. But buy a small number of well-shaped wineglasses. No one will enjoy Liebfraumilch⊕ served in a jelly glass.

Now comes the part that is really fun—setting the table. For a moment put out of your mind the memory of your mother calling you off the jungle gym to come home and set the table, and instead imagine yourself as a knowledgeable decorator ready to create a masterpiece.

⊕ Read: Chardonnay in today's world.

The focal point of your table need not be elaborate or expensive, but it should be colorful, interesting, and in keeping with the style of dinner you are serving. One rule to remember is this: no matter what you put in the center of your table, keep it low. You want him to be able to gaze into your baby blues, don't you?

Here are a few things we have used:

A white conch shell filled with colorful fruits (this might take care of dessert, too!).

For a very informal meal, you might pile a lettuce crisper or basket with colorful vegetables such as kale, eggplant, a head of cauliflower, artichokes, carrots, and beets.

If you have an eye for artistic arrangement, use a simple stark piece of driftwood from a day at the beach.

Pile up a pyramid of polished lemons and limes in a white bowl or wicker basket (they hold that shape miraculously if you stick them together with toothpicks).

Speaking of baskets, they come in such a variety of delightful sizes and shapes now—you should collect as many as you can afford. They will inspire an unlimited number of exciting centerpieces, and you'll find a million other uses for them too.

Here's one: use a long, low basket (the one you use for serving Italian bread). Snip a large bunch of grapes into smaller bunches. Use them to prop up a row of small candles in the basket. Slightly larger bunchlets are tucked around the candles and cascade over the sides of the basket.

Have you thought of using pinecones as candle or flower holders?

If you're planning a luau, use a pineapple as your centerpiece and surround it with flowers.

An attractive casserole dish can double as a vase if you fill it with lovely flowers. What about blue bachelor's buttons? They do have a certain social significance.

If you're having a seafood dinner, use the seafood itself as your centerpiece. Place a handsome king crab on a bed of escarole and garnish with radishes. A red lobster shell filled with green parsley will set off your seafood dinner beautifully.

While we're on the subject of using food as a centerpiece, we know a girl who is famous for her fabulous salads. And, you guessed it, they always repose in the place of honor.

If you don't want to fill your wooden salad bowl with lettuce, here are a few other things you can do with it: cut a piece of Styrofoam to fit the bottom of the bowl, and stick in some cattails, dried flowers, colorful autumn leaves, and dried cornhusks. You'll have an arrangement that will last until you're sick of it.

Fill the bowl with small pebbles and stones, and make a Japanese-style arrangement with a single graceful branch.

Put a pumpkin in the center of the bowl, and surround it with nuts and grapes for an autumn centerpiece.

Fill your polished wooden bowl with large scrubbed white mushrooms and nuts.

When you run out of ideas for things to do with your salad bowl, you might bring out another container and try making a bouquet of different shapes and colors of pasta. Your local Italian grocery will have the largest selection.

Instead of a single centerpiece, use a small nosegay of spring flowers or fresh green leaves in a low glass or egg cup at each place.

Use sugar bowls, pitchers, gravy boats, cups, or old copper pots for containers. You can browse around thrift shops for these. While you're there, you might even find an old hurricane lamp that makes a marvelous centerpiece.

The background of your table setting is as important as your centerpiece. Experiment with color combinations; try unusually colored and patterned tablecloths or mats. Even if you can't sew on a button, you can make some of these yourself just by fringing the edges. Don't be afraid of the unusual.

One of our favorite table settings was a cloth of black and white striped pillow ticking combined with bright red napkins. Try a flowered cloth combined with vivid napkins and plain dishes. Look for fabric with interesting texture, too—burlap is wonderful and cheap, cheap, cheap!

The main thing to remember when you are decorating your table and serving your food is this: don't be afraid to be unconventional, let your imagination run wild, and have fun. Your guests will, too.

3
Commonplace Cuisine

Quite frankly, we never worry very much about food. Usually we're either dieting or in the throes of a tragic love affair that requires some degree of sacrificial starvation. And when we're lucky, there are all of those lovely invitations: dinner at Ernie's, teas, showers, and Mother's good old pot roast on Sundays. Add to these the pretzels and peanuts that bartenders so thoughtfully provide and that dainty piece of chateaubriand smuggled home last night in a doggie bag, and we can pretty well get through the week without so much as a glance at the stove.

But no matter how carefully we plan things, there are always lean weeks, and we'll bet things aren't too different for you. Even if you have violet eyes and a figure to rival Miss de Milo, there are bound to be those inevitable evenings when that charmer in the accounting department doesn't give you a nod and even old Charlie's staying home tying trout flies. When it happens—and happen it will—just flip complacently to this chapter, secure in the knowledge that there is something here that is cheap and filling, quick to fix, and guaranteed not to give you botulism.

First of all, there is the old chop and steak gambit, which will always serve you in good stead. But a week of chops and steaks can do untold damage to your bank account besides being a bit of a bore. However, if you do happen to be blessed with a tender and succulent sirloin, it's a good idea to brush it with some Italian salad dressing or some soy sauce before you slide it under the broiler.♪ Nothing on which to build a reputation, mind you, but it does jazz it up.

However, when you're saving your pennies for that trip to Rome, there is always that old dependable:

The Daily Grind

Hamburgers are one of the basic facts of life, but there is no earthly reason why they have to taste like little wads of sawdust.

¼ pound ground round (if you're soloing tonight)
¼ teaspoon salt
Dash pepper
1 teaspoon onion flakes♪♪
Dash garlic salt

Mix ground round with salt, pepper, onion flakes, and garlic salt. Shape into one fat patty and slip it under the broiler. Keep poking to desired doneness.

♪ Remember that ridged stove-top grill pan back in chapter 1? Dust it off and use it. You'll never clean a greasy broiler again.

♪♪ Just mince a little of the real thing if you have the time—and the onion.

For a little variety, you can add to the basic recipe:

2 tablespoons toasted sesame seeds𝒹 (toast them in a 350° F.
   oven for 10–15 minutes), *or*
⅛ teaspoon dry mustard and a dash of nutmeg, *or*
¼ cup crushed potato chips, *or*
2 tablespoons sour cream, *or*
Some crumbled Roquefort cheese, *or*
If you cook the patty in a pan rather than in the broiler, pour
   on a little mushroom soup or wine during the last few minutes of cooking time.

If you're stuck for ideas about what to serve up with your tasty
hamburger, why not try one of the following? *Each recipe serves 1.*

Hamburger Haute Cuisine

Broil the hamburger 8–12 minutes, turning once.❓ Serve with:

Tomato halves: toss on some basil or other seasoning and broil
   15 minutes.
Mushroom caps: season well with salt and pepper, then broil
   15 minutes.
French bread slices: top with grated cheese and a little oregano;
   broil 1 minute or till golden.

𝒹 Buy these already toasted, freeing up 10 minutes to wash your hair.

❓ Hindsight would reveal that 12 minutes might render something
resembling a large piece of kibble. Check after 4 minutes per side.

It's obvious that you're going to have to do some fast footwork to get all those things in and out of the oven at the right time, but it's still easier than making hollandaise sauce.

Scramburgers

(When you have to eat and run)

Broil the patty 8–12 minutes.[?] Top a cooked potato (the leftover baked potato from last night's feast) with melted butter and seasoned salt or regular salt and pepper; broil 8 minutes. Broil canned cling peach or pear halves or pineapple chunks or slices for 8 minutes until golden.

Notice how cleverly everything works out if you like your hamburger rare?

DUCK SOUP

Let us turn for a moment to the subject of soup. Don't blanch. We are not for a moment suggesting that marvelous minestrone that takes all day to make and requires more than a nodding acquaintance with the art of seasoning plus a well-stocked stock pot. What we are suggesting is that when you come home beat after a long day at the water cooler, there is nothing so satisfying as a bowl of steaming soup. And if by chance it's a nice, filling concoction—well, there you are. The soups that we highly recommend are those with impeccable pedigrees that begin life

---

[?] See our revised cooking time on page 48.

in a spotless test kitchen and reach their final reward on your table, jazzed up with others of their stature and a lot of imagination. Just for a starter you might try:

Humbleburger Soup

Good for nights when you come home with your feet frozen and your nose a delicate mauve.

½ pound ground beef
1 tablespoon oil
1 small onion, chopped, or 1 teaspoon instant minced onion
½ cup water
½ package dry vegetable soup mix
½ cup chopped celery and leaves
½ can baked beans in tomato sauce̸ (or one small can)
¾ cup tomato juice

Shape ground beef into a large patty in a saucepan. Brown in oil 5 minutes on each side, then break up into chunks. Stir in

ᶜ Research has produced the distressing information that there are few surviving cans. Ms. Heinz is still putting up a few; if you can't find that, give it a shrug or be creative and throw in a can of garbanzos, black beans, or kidney beans. They're only beans, after all. Add a squirt of tomato paste from a handy tube, and you're off to the Culinary Institute.

onion and sauté until soft. Add water; heat to boiling; stir in soup mix and celery. Cover; cook 10 minutes. Stir in beans and tomato juice; heat slowly to boiling again and serve. *Serves 2.*

Something's Fishy

1 can condensed tomato soup
1 can condensed green pea soup
1 soup can water
1 cup milk
*1 can (about 5 ounces) deveined shrimps*ᵈ
½ teaspoon grated lemon rind

Combine soups, water, and milk in pot; heat and stir until blended. Rinse shrimps under running cold water, chop coarsely, and stir into soup. Heat just until bubbly hot; stir in lemon rind. Pour into heated soup bowls. *Serves 2.*

Lobster Bisque

1 can condensed cream of asparagus soup
1 can condensed cream of mushroom soup
1 soup can light cream
*1 can (6½ ounces) lobster meat*ᵈᵈ

ᵈ Salty, slippery shrimps from a can are not especially attractive. Pick up about 6 ounces of these baby crustaceans from the fishmonger.

ᵈᵈ Buy one small lobster tail and dice up the lobster meat. Or use quality canned lump crab (Phillips brand in a black can) and call it Crab Bisque.

Few grains cayenne
2 tablespoons sherry
2 tablespoons minced chives
Parmesan cheese croutons

Blend together soups, cream, lobster, and cayenne, and bring to a simmer. When mixture is hot, stir in sherry. Serve with a sprinkling of chives and Parmesan cheese croutons. *Serves 2.*

Cheater's Chowder

2 slices bacon, chopped
1 medium onion, chopped
1 can frozen condensed cream of potato soup,ᵟ thawed
Milk
1 can (7 ounces) minced clams
Pepper
Glob of butter

Fry the chopped bacon and onion together until the onion is flabby. Add milk to soup according to directions on can. Add the bacon and onion, clams, and pepper; simmer 12 minutes, and serve with that good fat chunk of butter floating in the middle. *Serves 2.*

ᵟ Canned frozen potato soup no longer exists in the freezer compartment. But Mother Campbell still makes cream of potato, bless her.

As you can see, soup is a perfectly delectable way of keeping body and soul together. With it you can have a nice green salad and crackers, French bread, English muffins, corn bread, or an old matzo.

Brave Old Bread

Here are a few things you can do to put a little pizzazz into:

English muffins: Split and spread surface with butter or margarine, top with one of these, then toast in broiler:

A few caraway, sesame, or poppy seeds
Some grated cheese—Swiss, Parmesan, or cheddar
A bit of curry powder
A sprinkle of dried thyme or dill

Hot dog buns:⊕ Slash each roll into five diagonal slices partway through. Butter cuts; in each, insert half slice of cheddar cheese and a thin onion slice. Bake at 425° F. for 10 minutes or until cheese melts; sprinkle with snipped parsley. Or quarter

---

⊕ This is quite embarrassing. When you think of it, today's world boasts loaves and loaves of crusty artisan breads, redolent of rosemary, kalamata olives, and roasted garlic. Slice them thick, acquaint them with olive oil, and warm them in the oven in foil, or throw them on your grill pan for a nice visual effect.

each roll *lengthwise* into four "bread sticks." Brush all over with salad oil. Sprinkle with one of the following, then toast in broiler:

Poppy or celery seeds
Snipped parsley or chives
Some caraway seeds
A few shakes of garlic, celery, or onion salt
A bit of dried rosemary or thyme

Split-top rolls: Partly separate "leaves" of brown-and-serve split-top rolls; spread with soft butter or margarine, then with one of these fillings:

Mayonnaise mixed with grated Parmesan cheese
Garlic salt plus mayonnaise
Mayonnaise plus curry powder and chopped mushrooms

Set on a baking sheet; bake according to directions on package.

If you want something a little more sturdy, try:

Pauper's Pizza

1 English muffin, split
1 dollop of tomato sauce
Pepperoni
1 slice mozzarella cheese (left over from last week's lasagna party)
Parmesan cheese
Oregano

Spread the English muffin with tomato sauce; place pepperoni, cheeses, and oregano on top. Slide under the broiler for about 1 minute or until cheese bubbles.

THE GOLDEN EYE

Let's not forget eggs. Even if you can't stand to have them staring you down at 7 in the morning, after you get home and settle down with a nice, wet martini, you may learn to love:

Bonanza Omelet

(In glorious living color)

3 eggs
¼ teaspoon salt
Dash pepper
2 tablespoons milk
1 can (2¼ ounces) deviled ham𝘥
2 tablespoons chopped onion
¼ small green pepper, diced
2 tablespoons butter or margarine

𝘥 You'd be better served to throw in a few thin strips of ham from the corner deli.

Beat eggs; add salt, pepper, milk, and ham; beat again. Stir in onion and green pepper. Heat butter or margarine in skillet over low heat; pour in egg mixture. Let omelet cook a minute or two. Run spatula around edge of pan, lifting edges of omelet to let uncooked egg mixture flow underneath. When eggs are cooked but still shiny, loosen omelet from pan with spatula, roll it or fold one half over the other, and turn it out onto your plate. *Serves 2.*

Devilish Scrambled Eggs

This is a good, quick *meal for one* when served with a salad and a selection of Brave Old Bread. When your roommate is home, too, just double the following:

> *3 well-beaten eggs*
> *¼ cup sour cream*
> *¼ teaspoon salt*
> *Dash pepper*
> *¼ teaspoon dry mustard*
> *2 tablespoons butter or margarine*

Combine eggs, sour cream, and seasonings. Heat butter in frying pan; pour in egg mixture and cook slowly until set, stirring frequently. You can add a can of mushrooms, some crumbled bacon, slivered salami, or a dab of spinach, cheese, rice, or just about anything else that you have hanging around the house to this delicious egg base. There are literally hundreds of variations to scrambled eggs, the very good and the very obvious being:

Crumbled bacon or leftover cubed ham
Sliced sautéed fresh mushrooms
Slivers of salami

But did you think of:

Chopped chives
Parmesan cheese[1]
Crumbled cream cheese[1]
Loads of cracked pepper and dill weed
Flaked crabmeat and curry powder[1]
Ricotta cheese and sliced Spanish olives
Cottage cheese[1]
Shredded cheddar cheese[1]
Crumbled Roquefort cheese
Just any old kind of cheese
2 heaping tablespoons parsley flakes[♪]
2 heaping tablespoons mustard or 1 tablespoon dry mustard
1 teaspoon tarragon
Sliced cocktail sausages
Shredded dried beef

Haven't you any imagination?

---

[1] Add when eggs are about 5 minutes from being done.

[♪] There are those annoying parsley flakes again. Shake the habit if you can.

CLASSY CASSEROLES

Now we come to those lifesavers—casseroles. When you're a working girl, they can be your best friend. We found that it was best to make them the night before while we were doing the dishes, bake them while we drooled over Dr. Kildare,⊕ and park them in the refrigerator to be reheated the next night. Most of the following recipes are for two—you and your roommate. If, however, you live alone, you can always freeze the leftovers for a later feast.

Our Wild Irish Stew

½ pound ground beef
1 tablespoon fat∂
1 medium onion, sliced thin
½ cup shredded cabbage
¼ cup diced celery
1 cup red kidney beans
¼ cup cooked canned tomatoes
Salt and pepper
½ teaspoon chili powder
1 cup instant mashed potatoes∂∂

⊕ See note on page 6.

∂ *Fat* is an ugly word. Think thin; Pam spray is kinder to your waistline.

∂∂ Go ahead—just hide the telltale box underneath the coffee grounds!

Brown ground beef in hot fat. Add onion, cabbage, and celery, and cook until vegetables are yellow. Add beans, tomatoes, salt, pepper, and chili powder. Add water to cover (about 1½ cups) and simmer 15 minutes. Prepare instant mashed potatoes according to the instructions on the package. Serve stew in bowls and top with mashed potatoes. *Serves 2.*

Crabby Casserole

This one is definitely good enough for company. But it's also dandy for pampering yourself when you have the sniffles and the world is out to get you.

   1 can (7½ ounces) king crabmeat♪
   2 tablespoons butter or margarine
   2 tablespoons unsifted flour
   1 teaspoon salt
   Pinch pepper
   ½ teaspoon paprika
   1 teaspoon instant minced onion♪♪
   1¾ cups milk
   ¾ cup macaroni shells

♪ Use only best-quality lump crabmeat. Look for Phillips in a 1-pound can. You'll have to have crab salad for lunch and crab enchiladas for dinner, but it's worth it.

♪♪ You know how we feel about this. See note on page 7.

½ package frozen artichoke hearts⁄
3 tablespoons sherry
½ cup grated sharp cheddar cheese

Flake the crabmeat with a fork and set aside. Melt butter in a
saucepan and remove from heat. Stir in flour, salt, pepper, and
paprika to make a smooth mixture. Add onion and gradually stir
in milk. Bring to a boil and then reduce heat. Simmer 5 minutes, then remove from heat and put it somewhere out of the
way while you cook the macaroni and artichoke hearts as the
labels direct (in separate pans, of course). Drain both well.
Combine crabmeat, sherry, macaroni, and artichoke hearts with
the sauce. Mix the whole thing up and put in a casserole dish.
Place tenderly in the refrigerator until your stomach starts to
growl.† Then sprinkle the top with cheese and bake 20 minutes
(350° F.) until bubbly. *Serves 2–3* hungry people and can easily
be doubled.

Chicken La Bodega

For one summer this was the only dish we ever served to guests,
and strangely enough they never got tired of it. We can't say the
same, however. Fortunately, enough time has passed so that

⁄ There are high-quality precooked artichoke hearts in cans today.
Be sure you don't buy the marinated ones in glass jars for this
particular recipe.

we can once again look a chicken squarely in the eye without flinching.

1 package chicken pieces (frozen fryer)ᶝ
1 teaspoon salt
1 teaspoon paprika
⅓ cup olive oil
3 tablespoons butter
¼ teaspoon saffron (distressingly expensive but lasts forever)
1 cup uncooked rice
1 cup white wine
1 cup chicken stock
Bay leaves
½ cup ripe olives, pitted
1 package frozen peas

You should be able to find frozen chicken parts in your market; otherwise your butcher will gladly clean and cut up a fryer for you. When you have finally found your chicken and safely guided it home, pat it with a damp paper towel. Season with salt and paprika. Brown slowly in olive oil. In another pan, melt butter and stir in saffron and rice. Toast rice in frying pan until golden brown, stirring occasionally for about 10 minutes. Add white wine and chicken stock; simmer covered for about

---

ᶝ Fresh chicken would be much better here or anywhere. Look for a cut-up fryer or just go with those male favorites, breasts and thighs.

15 minutes. Place bay leaves on bottom of casserole. Add rice, chicken, and olives. Bake for 40 minutes in 350° F. oven.† Add 1 package cooked frozen peas and heat in 350° oven. This recipe *serves 4*, but if there are going to be only two of you for dinner, make the whole thing, for the leftovers freeze well in a tightly sealed container.

Cha Cha Enchiladas

This is not really a refrigerator dish, but it is so easy and good that we just couldn't leave it out—so get out your castinets and go to work.

> 2 medium onions, chopped
> Salad oil⁄
> 1 pound ground round
> 1 clove garlic
> Salt and pepper
> Chili powder (the amount is left to your discretion and the sensi-
> tivity of your taste buds, but make it at least 1½ tablespoons)
> ¾ cup tomatoes or ¾ cup water (water makes the chili hotter)
> Oregano
> 6 tortillas
> Grated yellow cheddar cheese

⁄ See our discussion of the oil business in chapter 1. You'll need canola oil for this recipe.

Cook half the onion in oil until transparent, then add beef and garlic. Salt and pepper heavily, and add as much chili powder as you can stand. Add either the water or the tomatoes. Simmer until gloppy. Add oregano and simmer some more. Sizzle the tortillas in a frying pan coated with oil for a minute or two. Spread each with some of the beef mixture and roll them up. Lay side by side in a shallow casserole and throw on the rest of the meat mixture. Sprinkle with grated cheese and remaining chopped onion. Bake in a 350° F. oven until cheese melts, about 15 minutes. Great with a tall, cold beer. *Serves 2.*

4

Food Fit for a . . .

Nothing sends a girl into a tizzy as fast as the realization that she must cook dinner for a man. Even if she was born with a wooden spoon in her hand, she will probably not be able to manage the evening without the aid of some strong smelling salts and a few belts of the cooking sherry. Knowing, as we do, the horrors of such occasions, we have tried to patch together memories of some of our more distinguished feasts in the hope that they will be of some assistance to you in your hour of greatest need.

You will notice that we have blithely categorized men in what some would feel was an overly simplified fashion. But, as you probably have already discovered, each wily man, though he tries valiantly to pass himself off as a unique individual, is actually just a member of an easily defined type. And for each category of men, there is a perfect menu. So have a swig of that cooking sherry and relax.

Food Fit for a . . .
Man in a Brooks Brothers Suit

In every big city there are literally thousands of this breed running around loose. They are usually found at lunchtime sipping martinis in dimly lit bars or dreaming of new ways to rise to the top of the Madison Avenue ladder. They are equally recognizable on weekends: driving small red sports cars, sailing or skiing, sipping Irish coffee, or perusing the centerfold of a men's magazine.

Jinx's Brooks Brothers bachelor was a natty young man named Bryan, who could have glibly planned a successful campaign to sell surfboards to midwesterners.

When you meet your Bryan and are ready to start an all-out campaign, here is a menu well tailored to your purposes. Remember that this is not the time for your mother's yummy scalloped potatoes. It was probably those very scalloped potatoes that drove him from the comforts of his mother's hearth in Sheboygan.

If you can cook without tripping over it, by all means wear your chicest hostess skirt.☺ This is known as packaging the product. Pile your hi-fi☺☺ with soft, seductive jazz and bring out all the candles you can hunt up. Now cross his palm with a martini, and when he is sufficiently soothed, run this up the flagpole and just watch him salute it!

☺ A fashion as antiquated as the hi-fi we're about to mention.

☺☺ Once thought to be the ultimate in sound equipment. Much larger than an iPod.

FLAWLESS FONDUE
SPINACH AND BACON SALAD
STRAWBERRIES AND KIRSCH
RIESLING

Flawless Fondue⊕

½ loaf French or Italian bread
1 clove garlic, split
¾ pound Swiss cheese, grated
Dash salt and pepper
Dry white wine
3 tablespoons cornstarch
1 tablespoon kirsch
1 tablespoon water

Cut loaf of bread into cubes (having a little crust on each cube) early in the day. Set out on cookie sheet so that it will get slightly hard. Use deep baking dish or crockery utensil (not metal). Rub sides with garlic. Put cheese, salt, and pepper into dish, and add enough wine to barely cover. Cook over medium heat and stir constantly, heating just until cheese melts—no longer. Cheese and wine will not be blended yet.

Make a smooth paste of cornstarch, kirsch, and water. Stir cornstarch mixture into cheese and wine. Cook over medium

---

⊕ Fondue took a sabbatical for a couple of decades, but it's back in style now, and fondue pots abound in most culinary catalogs.

heat and stir until mixture is about as thick as a medium cream sauce. *Serves 2.* Serve bubbling hot in a prewarmed chafing dish or crockery dish. Fondue forks are ideal and not very expensive, but you can use those long Japanese hors d'oeuvre sticks.

There's a delightful tradition that goes with fondue, and if you're brazen enough, you really ought to introduce it. If a lady drops her bread, she must kiss the gentleman on her right, and if a man drops his bread, he must drain his glass. Since there are only two of you, you'd better spear that bread with a steady hand.

Spinach and Bacon Salad

DRESSING:
Combine the following and let stand for 30 minutes before adding to greens.

1 small clove garlic, sliced
¼ cup olive oil
1 teaspoon sugar
¾ teaspoon oregano
1 teaspoon salt
⅛ teaspoon pepper
1 tablespoon wine vinegar
2 tablespoons lemon juice

Remove garlic before adding to greens.

SALAD:
6 slices bacon
1 head Belgian endive, torn
¼ pound crisp raw spinach, torn

Fry bacon until crisp; drain and crumble when cool. Sprinkle over greens and toss with dressing when ready to serve. *Serves 2 generously.*

Strawberries and Kirsch

(Or May wine)

Find the most voluptuous strawberries around, rinse, and take those little green things off the end. Drain; place, covered, in refrigerator until ready to serve. Drizzle kirsch or May wine over the berries until they're standing in approximately ½ inch of the wine. Delightful!

Food Fit for a . . .

Man's Man

The man's man is something of a vanishing breed—like the whooping crane. Judy met hers one summer while she was vacationing in the mountains. He was a forest ranger named Eric who tended toward plaid wool shirts, khakis, and desert boots and smoked only Marlboros.⊕ He was really quite impressive in his

---

⊕ That was considered very cool long ago.

native habitat, but when he came tooling up to our San Francisco apartment in a forest green pickup truck with a dead elk slung on top, a little of the shine seemed to go out of Judy's eyes.

However, if you are an outdoor girl, the man's man is the man for you. Catch him between seasons (duck and deer) and he will adore a home-cooked dinner. Under no circumstances fix him any sort of game lest he take it upon himself to keep your freezer stocked forevermore with unplucked, uncleaned, unfortunate little birds and beasts. He'll enjoy a nice rare steak nearly as much, and the future of your freezing compartment will be more secure. Remember—nothing fancy for the man's man. Keep everything as close to Nature's intention as possible.

SURLY STEAK

ONE MAN'S ORIGINAL STEAK MARINADE

GNOCCHI À LA ROMANA

(OR BAKED POTATO FOR THE PURIST)

GREEN SALAD

CHOCOLATE FUDGE CAKE

CABERNET SAUVIGNON

Surly Steak

General directions for broiling a steak:

1. Buy a good piece of meat (sirloin, filet, etc.) from your twinkly-eyed butcher and then treat it with tender loving care.

2. Have the steak at room temperature. Preheat broiler and broiler pan,♥ with rack 3–4 inches from heat.

3. Trim a little fat from steak: use to rub over broiler rack, or brush rack with a little oil.

4. Broil steak on one side; season with salt and pepper. Turn steak with tongs; broil on other side.

5. To test for doneness, cut small slit in meat near bone or in center. Broil longer if meat is too rare. Season with salt and pepper. Serve on a hot platter with canned mushroom sauce, if you like.

6. If you're really a smart girl and have invested in a small newspaper-burning grill, you can just hand Eric the comic section and shove him out the door. This is by far the easiest way.

One Man's Original Steak Marinade

If you are going to barbecue on your outdoor grill, here is a marinade that our downstairs neighbor has petulantly insisted we include. He claims it is his very own bachelor invention, and in all honesty it is quite good.

♥ Use the ridged grill pan we told you about in chapter 1, or if you found that elusive apartment-size barbecue, haul that out to the balcony.

2 large onions, sliced thin
3 cloves garlic
½ cup olive oil
2 tablespoons garlic wine vinegar
Juice of 1 lemon
Cracked Java pepper
Pinch thyme
Pinch oregano
Bay leaves
Good red wine

Place half of the sliced onion in bottom of a shallow pan. Crush garlic cloves and mix with all other ingredients except wine. Put steaks on top of onions and pour sauce over all. Add wine to cover steaks. Put the rest of the onions on top and cover. Let stand for several hours.

Gnocchi à la Romana?

2 cups milk
½ cup butter, divided
½ cup hominy grits (not quick-cooking variety)
½ teaspoon salt

? This bears no resemblance to Italian gnocchi, but Jinx's aunt Ruth called it that and we didn't want to question her on the point. With the unusual inclusion of grits we should, perhaps, have called it Nashville Nocchi. Whatever you call it, it's yummy.

Pinch pepper
½ cup grated Gruyère or Swiss cheese
¼ cup Parmesan cheese

Bring milk to a boil. Add ¼ cup butter cut in pieces to melt. Gradually stir in hominy grits. Continue stirring and cooking until mixture looks like cooked mush. Remove from heat, season with salt and pepper, and beat hard with mixer until creamy. Pour into square pan to set. Cut into rectangular pieces. Place in serving dish like fallen dominoes. Pour ¼ cup melted butter over and sprinkle cheeses on top. Heat in 400° F. oven for 30–35 minutes. *Serves 2*.

If you have a real man's man on your hands, he'll probably turn up his nose at anything as exotic as Gnocchi à la Romana, in which case he ought to have his nose examined. But if such is the case, fix baked potatoes according to the directions in your big fat cookbook. And hide your sour cream—he doesn't deserve it.

Green Salad

DRESSING:
¼ cup salad oil☙
3 tablespoons tomato juice
1 tablespoon fresh lemon juice
1 teaspoon grated or scraped onion

☙ Per our discussion in chapter 1, this is the time to use good-quality olive oil.

¼ *teaspoon salt*
¼ *teaspoon black pepper*
¼ *teaspoon sugar*
¼ *teaspoon crumbled, dried sweet basil*

Shake together in a jar; let stand and blend together.

SALAD:
1 head Boston lettuce, torn
Add to the lettuce:
⅓ *cup coarsely broken walnuts, slightly*
   toasted in 400° F. oven for a few minutes
¼ *cup grated Parmesan cheese*

Pour salad dressing over lettuce, walnuts, and cheese. Toss and serve at once. *Serves 2* famished diners.

Chocolate Fudge Cake

That towering, toothsome Chocolate Fudge Cake is magically made from a mix—but you get all the credit.

Food Fit for a . . .
Man in a Garret

During our Edna St. Vincent Millay period, we met a charming young man named Jonathan. He was easy enough to spot—the only one in the crowd with shaggy hair, a clay pipe, *and* a wine-red velvet smoking jacket. He always came to our door bearing a bouquet of snow crocuses and a slim volume of obscure poetry. He was, indeed, a bright light in our drab existence.

If you should meet a Jonathan, treat him tenderly, for he will depend on you to breathe life into his genius. To be specific, he will depend on you to feed him about once a week. Here's a menu he'll love: it's straight out of the Barretts of Wimpole Street, and it will perk him up if he has just received his one thousandth rejection slip or if his tabby cat recently tipped over a can of turpentine on his newest canvas.

ROCOCO CORNISH GAME HENS
IMPRESSIONIST GREEN RICE
SCULPTOR'S SALAD WITH SOUR CREAM
BAROQUE CHERRIES JUBILEE
DRY SAUVIGNON BLANC,
GREY RIESLING, OR BURGUNDY
(IF YOU LIKE RED WINE WITH GAME BIRDS)

Rococo Cornish Game Hens

2 1-pound Rock Cornish hens
3 tablespoons butter
½ cup minced onion
1 can (6 ounces) sliced broiled-in-butter mushrooms♀

♀ Fresh, please! Wipe with a damp cloth (don't wash) and slice. Oh, and did we tell you to thaw those hapless birds first? Do.

¾ cup white wine or chicken broth
2 tablespoons cornstarch
¼ cup cold water
1 teaspoon gravy color enhancer⌀
1 cup sour cream

Cut the hens in half, using sharp kitchen shears (those are the ones you cut your bangs with). Melt butter in skillet; add hens, skin side down, and add the onion. Sauté about 10 minutes. Drain mushrooms, saving the broth, and add just the wine or broth to the hens.† Lower heat; cover and simmer 30 minutes. Remove hens from skillet and place on warm serving platter. Combine cornstarch, cold water, and color enhancer; stir into pan drippings. Cook, stirring constantly, until gravy thickens and is smooth. Stir in sour cream and mushrooms, and heat gently until piping hot. Do not allow to boil. Pour directly over hens on serving plates.

Impressionist Green Rice

1½ cups cooked rice
¾ cup minced parsley
½ cup grated yellow cheese
½ medium onion, chopped

⌀ All this does is make sauces a prettier shade of tan. Look for Bovril or Kitchen Bouquet.

1 *cup milk*
1 *slightly beaten egg*
Salt and pepper
½ *cup salad oil*❓

Mix everything but the salad oil thoroughly. Place in a casserole and pour the oil over. Cook uncovered for 40 minutes in a 375° F. oven. *Serves 2.*

Sculptor's Salad with Sour Cream

Tear up whatever greens you have on hand. Add sliced tomato or what you will. Sprinkle generously with salt, Java cracked black pepper, and frozen chives.† When ready to serve, toss with sour cream.❦

Baroque Cherries Jubilee

1 *can (16 ounces) pitted black cherries*
1 *cup juice from cherries*
3 *ounces brandy*
Vanilla ice cream

❓ A recent run-through in our Caribbean test kitchen revealed that 2 tablespoons of canola or olive oil would be quite enough, thank you.

❦ We're inclined to add a splash of balsamic vinegar just to smooth things out a bit. Otherwise, the sour cream might appear to be ice floes marooned atop the lettuce.

Saving the juice, drain cherries. Pour back 1 cup of juice to cover them. Heat. Add heated brandy and set afire, stirring and dipping the liquid over the cherries until flames die out. Serve over vanilla ice cream immediately. *Serves 2.*

Food Fit for a . . .
Lover with a Leica

Our hometown Clark Kent, when he wasn't chasing ambulances or stirring up union leaders, always had a habit of dropping in just at dinnertime. His reasoning was not altogether illogical: reporters are notoriously underpaid and usually underweight. But he always held up his part of the unspoken bargain by forcing us into heated political arguments and by keeping us up on all the local gossip around the Civic Center.

Since your reporter will probably appear on a fairly regular schedule, complete with that hungry look, we have chosen a menu that, though spartan in appearance, is actually very filling and will be a delight to your budget. It will also add a bit of atmosphere, since it will take your boy journalist forward to the day when he will grab a quick bite in the U.S. Senate Dining Room just before rushing out to cover a national crisis. While the beans are brewing, you'll have time to do your nails and catch up on what Walter Lippmann and Joseph Alsop⊕ are saying.

⊕ Well, these guys were *old* when we wrote this book the *first* time. But homage is due to two of America's venerated journalists. Today, you might think of Woodward and Bernstein.

SENATE BEAN SOUP
WILTED SPINACH SALAD
GARLIC BREAD
FRUIT AND CHEESE
DANISH BEER

We once saw a recipe for the famous bean soup that is served in the Senate Dining Room. We searched diligently through what we laughingly call our "recipe file," but to no avail. We finally found it in a shoe box under the bed. So here it is, a bit dusty, but hardly worse for the wear.

Senate Bean Soup

1 cup navy beans
1½ quarts water
1 meaty ham bone or ham hock
¼ cup instant mashed potatoes⌀
½ cups finely chopped onions
3 finely chopped celery stalks with leaves
1 clove garlic, pressed
⅛ cup finely chopped parsley
Salt and pepper to taste

⌀ This is one cheat we'll let you get away with. It's just there to thicken the soup.

Soak beans overnight in water. Add ham bone,♨ cover, and simmer until beans are just beginning to soften (about 1 hour). Add mashed potatoes and stir until smooth. Add onion, celery, garlic, and parsley, and simmer another hour until beans are soft. Add more water if needed, but soup should be very thick. Season to taste with salt and pepper.† *Should serve about 4*, but our friend used to be able to finish the pot.

Wilted Spinach Salad

1 bunch spinach
2 slices bacon, semicooked
¼ cup wine vinegar
½ cup olive oil
1 teaspoon Worcestershire sauce
Salt and pepper
1 chopped hard-cooked egg

Wash and drain spinach thoroughly. Cut bacon into 1-inch pieces, and place in frying pan with small amount of oil. Cook until bacon is crisp. Add vinegar, oil, Worcestershire, salt, and pepper. Pour above dressing over spinach and mix thoroughly. (Mixture must be piping hot to wilt the spinach and give it a tender texture.) Place in individual salad bowls and sprinkle lightly with the chopped egg. *Serves 2*.

♨ We neglected to mention that in polite circles, the ham bone is removed to the dog's dish before ladling out this hearty repast.

Garlic Bread

You're really missing something if you don't know how to make garlic bread. We used to live on the stuff. There are three ways to make garlic bread. The third is the only sensible course of action, but we thought you'd like to know the others in case anyone is so gauche as to ask for your recipe.

1. *Legitimate Garlic Bread:* Mince 1–2 cloves garlic or put through a garlic press. Sauté in melted butter, strain, and brush in crevices of a loaf of French bread that has been sliced almost all the way through.

2. *Stepchild Garlic Bread:* Melt ¼–½ pound butter and ¼–½ teaspoon garlic powder. Allow flavors to mingle for about 5 minutes. Follow same procedure as in Legitimate Garlic Bread.

3. *Cheater's Garlic Bread:* Buy a good packaged garlic spread at the market. Follow the directions on jar. *Magnifique!* No one will know you've cheated, so don't breathe a word—literally.❓

Fruit and Cheese

Being trusting souls, we leave the decision up to you as to what kinds of fruit and cheese you will serve. Perhaps the most impor-

---

❓ Oh, shame. Get a grip on your garlic press, soften some butter, and make the real thing. If you must indulge in chicanery, melt some butter, throw in some Penzeys (see chapter 1 again!) garlic salt, and let 'er rip.

tant element in serving fruit and cheese for dessert is the serving itself. We hope your aesthetic sense will prevent you from thrusting an apple and a tired hunk of cheddar under the poor fellow's nose.

In the very posh circles (or so they tell us), it's considered highly proper to select just one perfect piece of fruit per guest. But to get away with anything that simple, you really must have a lovely Steuben dessert plate on which to place each solitary piece of Nature's effort. You can solve this problem by arranging a mass of fruit in the center of the table. This provides a centerpiece as well as dessert.

A tray or serving platter piled high with oversize grapes, pears, and oranges whisked from the refrigerator to the table provides a delightful dessert when accompanied by one or two good cheeses.

Rich, creamy cheeses are the perfect complement to fresh fruit. Some of the best are Brie, Camembert, Pont l'Evêque, Bel Paese, or Taleggio. The best Brie and Camembert come from France, although some very good ones are made in America. Pont l'Evêque is always imported from France, and Bel Paese is a creamy Italian cheese. Taleggio is a mild but rich cheese that also originates in Italy. Any of these cheeses should be served with melba toast or thinly sliced French bread. Just avoid crackers that are salted, since cheeses are already quite salty.

Other good fruit-cheese combinations you might try are Liederkranz with Tokay grapes, blue or Roquefort with pears, Roquefort with fresh kumquats, and Camembert with tart plums and cracked walnuts.

Food Fit for a . . .
Man in the Gray Flannel Lederhosen

At one point in our career we made the acquaintance of a real live Jet-Setter. If the truth be known, it was Judy's conquest, and she was the envy of every girl who ever read *Vogue*. The romance perked along quite well for several months until the evening that she decided she must have him over to dinner. The following menu is a re-creation of that fateful evening. She felt that if she offered him something faintly reminiscent of exotic ports of call, he might be convinced that all that roaming was unnecessary when he could get the same things so close to home. The dinner was a triumph, but the evening, his image, and the romance started to fall apart when this glamorous creature subjected us to his complete repertoire of double-exposed *home movies!*

However, if you happen to know a world traveler, whether airline pilot, bon vivant, or traveling salesman (oh, really . . .), this menu should stand you in good stead. Need we add that you should invite this fleet-footed creature only if your intentions are serious. Anyone who can afford a round-trip ticket to anywhere these days can certainly treat you to Tournedos Rossini and has no right to take advantage of your warmhearted hospitality.

One more note: if your wayfarer dominates the conversation with thrilling tales of his travels, punctuated by out-of-focus home movies, your only social obligation is to keep from yawning . . . or at least cover your mouth.

PHILEAS FOGG'S WORLDLY STROGANOFF
WILD RICE
SPECIAL SALAD
SWEDISH CREAM
CABERNET SAUVIGNON

Beef by any other name should taste as good. . . .

Phileas Fogg's Worldly Stroganoff

4 tablespoons flour, divided
½ teaspoon salt
1 pound top sirloin cut in ½-inch strips
4 tablespoons butter, divided
1 cup sliced fresh mushrooms
½ cup chopped onion
1 clove garlic, put through press or minced if you're a diehard
1 tablespoon tomato paste
1 can beef consommé♥
1 cup sour cream
2 tablespoons sherry

Combine 1 tablespoon flour and salt; roll meat strips in mixture. Melt 2 tablespoons butter in a skillet, add sirloin, and brown

---

♥ The soup section of your supermarket has many kinds of stock—beef, chicken, vegetable—that can be reconstituted, a tablespoon or a cup at a time. The flavors are truer and don't resemble a lab experiment gone awry.

on all sides. Add mushrooms, onion, and garlic; cook until onion is barely tender—about 5 minutes.

Remove meat and mushrooms temporarily from pan; melt 2 tablespoons butter in pan drippings and add 3 tablespoons flour, stirring to avoid lumps. Add tomato paste. Pour in consommé and cook, stirring constantly until mixture thickens. Return meat and mushrooms to skillet.† Stir in sour cream and sherry; heat thoroughly but don't boil. Serve at once. This actually *makes 3–4 servings*, but once again, the leftovers are great.

Wild Rice

Drain juice from canned wild rice and heat with lots of butter. *Makes 1 serving per can.*❢

❢ Someone should have held our heads underwater in a distant rice paddy when we even gave voice to this idea. So, blushing over, here's the simplest and best method for cooking wild rice. It's no longer a budget buster either, so march down that aisle and snag a bag of Minnesotan manna. Some rice kernels are harder than others, so the timing will have to be part of your sentinel duty. So, here goes:

Rinse 1 cup rice in a strainer; place in heavy 3-quart pan with 2½–3 cups unsalted chicken broth. Cover and bring to a boil for 10 minutes. Reduce heat; simmer for about 50 minutes. Check for tenderness near the end of the cooking time. Salt as needed. *Makes about 3 cups.* Leftovers freeze happily in sealable plastic bags.

We have blithely mentioned "tossed green salad," yet never have we been so generous as to give you our recipe for the greatest tossed green salad. If you just sit tight, we'll share with you a recipe for the king of all salads; but forgive us if, for a moment, we digress on the beauties of the salad.

A good, hearty, unafraid salad speaks worlds for your prowess as a cook, besides making pasty old vegetables take a backseat forever. Even for your weekday meals, a salad will accompany whatever else is on the table *d'hôte,* and you can justifiably turn the other cheek when those frozen broccoli spears snarl at you from your freezing compartment with the ferocity of a doting mother.

One sturdy piece of advice: get yourself a favorite salad, and serve it over and over again to your guests. Chances are they'll never know, but if they do, they'll forgive you if it's a very special one. A large repertoire of salads doesn't do anyone any good, but one or two perfected bowls from the garden will bring you laurels. The following green salad is a terror to prepare, but we hope you'll have the courage to try it.

Special Salad

1 tablespoon olive oil
Salt
1 clove garlic
1 head romaine lettuce, torn
1 tomato, peeled and cut in eighths
3–4 green onions, chopped

¼ *cup grated Parmesan or Romano cheese*
6 *slices bacon, cooked and crumbled*

Rub a large wooden bowl with olive oil, sprinkle of salt, and
garlic. Toss out the garlic and place all ingredients in the bowl.
Add croutons if you like, pour dressing (below) over all, and toss
knowledgeably.

DRESSING:
1½ *ounces olive oil*
Juice of 1 lemon
Fat pinch oregano
Dash cracked pepper
1 *coddled egg*

In a small jar, mix all dressing ingredients except the coddled
egg. Add the egg (a coddled egg is one that's been placed in sim-
mering hot water for 1½–2 minutes) and shake with fervor.

Swedish Cream

1 *cup plus 3 tablespoons heavy cream*
½ *cup sugar*
1 *envelope plain gelatin*
½ *pint sour cream*
½ *teaspoon vanilla*
1 *package frozen raspberries*

Mix heavy cream, sugar, and gelatin, and heat gently until gelatin is completely dissolved. Cool on back of stove until slightly thickened. Fold in sour cream and flavor with vanilla. Try to prevent lumps, but don't lose any sleep if you see a few, as they'll get lost in the shuffle anyway. Chill until firm. Spoon into serving dishes and top with raspberries. Double-rich. You can make this in the morning, but don't try to do it the night before, as you run the risk of it separating into something like the Grand Canyon. *Serves 4* if you don't snitch.

Food Fit for a . . .
Man with a Million

Liz, the girl upstairs, came crashing in one evening to announce loudly that she had met and wooed Mr. Bucks himself and he was coming to dinner. She considered it a delightful prospect until we opined as how Scott was probably weaned on fine imported wines and had passed up Pablum for chocolate mousse. What's more, he wasn't apt to fall into ecstasies over Prospector's Beans* or even a three-inch sirloin.

After Liz recovered from her decline, the three of us conjured up a menu that sent Scott home fat and happy, certain that he had found a real prize. We decided that the secret lies in whipping up something that not even the Pump Room has on the bill of fare. This does not mean dreaming up an "original" casserole of cashew nuts and ground round smothered with hollandaise. It does call for a real delicacy, concocted without concern for the cost of ingredients—thereby indicating that money is no object for you, either, and that you're certainly not after him for his granddaddy's coupons.

If you have a jewel of a roommate, she might condescend to being locked in the kitchen all evening where she would emit loud clatterings of pots and pans and guttural mutterings. When asked, you may refer to her with an airy wave of the hand as your "girl" Bertha. To prevent discovery, tell him you prefer to do the serving this evening as you bring in:

OPULENT CHICKEN

WILD RICE   GREEN SALAD

ABIE'S IRISH COFFEE   DATES AND NUTS

CHABLIS OR GREY RIESLING

Opulent Chicken

This will serve more than two,? but the leftovers are equally as good as the beginners.

4 complete chicken breasts
Paprika
Salt

? Well, no kidding. It'll serve 8, as written, so at least cut down on the amount of chicken. Who cares if there's a lot of sauce??

Pepper
¼ *pound (1 stick) butter*
1 *can (15 ounces) artichoke hearts*
½ *pound fresh mushrooms, sliced*
1 *pinch tarragon*
3 *tablespoons flour*
⅓ *cup sherry*
1½ *cups chicken bouillon*

Split the chicken breasts and slather them with the paprika, salt, and pepper. Sauté in ½ stick butter until golden brown. Place the chicken pieces in a large serving casserole and add the artichokes among them. Put the mushrooms and the remaining half of the butter in the same skillet you used for browning the chicken. Season with the tarragon and sauté for about 5 minutes. Sprinkle the flour in gently, and add the sherry and bouillon. Simmer for 5 minutes and pour this sauce over the chicken and artichokes. Cover the casserole and bake for 45 minutes at 375° F. *Serves 4.*

Wild Rice

Open a can, drain off excess juice, heat, and toss with lots of butter.❣

❣ For shame! See note on page 86.

Green Salad

Try Château Salad.*

Abie's Irish Coffee⊕

Whip cream to the consistency of thick cake batter. Into an Irish coffee glass or a wineglass, pour 1 heaping tablespoon sugar, followed by steaming hot coffee. Add 1 ounce Irish whiskey and top with ½ inch of the semiwhipped cream. Imbibe.

Dates and Nuts

Have a gleaming plate of plump, pitted dates and burnished pecans ready to serve with the Irish coffee.

Food Fit for a . . .
Gallant Gourmet

There was a charming man who used to work in the accounting department who had a real penchant for exotic food. Dear Lester couldn't see either one of us for sour apples, but when it

---

⊕ Our recent research has shown that Irish coffee, whether in a pub in Kilkenny or on your own back porch, satisfies the four necessary food groups: sugar, fat, alcohol, and caffeine. You needn't share that thought with your personal trainer.

came to filling in that last hungry gap before payday, he was always there with an attractive invitation. He squired us all over San Francisco trying everything from Sub Gum Yuk to Fromage Glace.

An overexuberant moment of camaraderie caused us to pause over Bombay Duck one night and invite Lester to dinner. Pure buffoonery on our part. Until now our gourmet friend had been a delightful companion and escort, for having dinner with a man who treasures good food is a real treat. But now the enormity of our folly hit us. Suppose the meal were really terrible? He might be disappointed; worse yet, he conceivably could decide to adopt some other hungry girls. Our number was up; we were forced into the kitchen with knees trembling as we prepared to make like Escoffier.⊕

If it happens to you, take heart, for here is a menu even Lester didn't resist. Any gourmet worth his chocolate-covered ladybugs dotes on seafood laced with sherry and a subtle cream sauce. You won't have to worry about conversation or candlelight; simply paste on your best and bravest smile as you lead him to the slaughter.

⊕ See note on page 28.

HEARTS OF PALM SALAD
LOBSTER THERMIDOR
CURRIED RICE   CHUTNEY
FRUIT AND CHEESE
COFFEE   BRANDY
LIEBFRAUMILCH♥

Hearts of Palm Salad

1 *head iceberg lettuce,ℰ torn*
1 *avocado, peeled and diced*
1 *can (14 ounces) hearts of palm, drained and sliced ¼ inch thick*
2 *tablespoons vinegar*
⅓ *cup salad oil♥♥*
Salt and pepper

Throw lettuce, avocado (gently), and hearts of palm into salad bowl. In a small jar, combine vinegar, salad oil, salt, and pepper; shake well, pour over salad, toss, and *serve to 2.*

♥ Pick up a bottle of Chardonnay instead—much easier to find *and* pronounce.

ℰ The palette will be more appealing to the palate if you substitute darker-leaved lettuces or romaine.

♥♥ Olive oil! We keep telling you!

Lobster Thermidor

3 8-ounce frozen rock lobster tails♥
Boiling water
3 tablespoons butter or margarine
2 tablespoons all-purpose flour
Pinch nutmeg
Paprika
½ teaspoon salt
1½ tablespoons sherry
1 cup light cream
¼ cup grated cheddar cheese

Early in the morning while you're hanging your hair out to dry, you can toss the lobster tails in boiling salted water, allowing 3 minutes longer than the ounce weight of the largest tail (for example, 11 minutes for 8-ounce tails). Drain and cool. Snip away thin underside membrane and pull out meat with fingers. Cut lobster meat in chunks. Wash shells and stash everything in the refrigerator.† About an hour before serving, melt butter in your double boiler; stir in flour, nutmeg, dash paprika, salt, and sherry. Slowly add cream, stirring constantly. Add lobster chunks; cook over hot water, stirring occasionally, till just thickened. Fill shells with lobster mixture. Sprinkle each with cheese and then lightly with paprika. Just before serving, heat

---

♥ Opt for an equal weight of fresh lobster tails if available.

broiler for about 10 minutes. Arrange filled lobster shells in foil-lined pan, and broil until just golden on top. Arrange lobster on serving platter around center mound of Curried Rice. *Serves 2.*

Curried Rice

Butter or margarine
1 cup uncooked white rice
1½ teaspoons curry powder
1 medium onion, minced
2 cups boiling water
Chutney

Heat oven to 400° F. Brown rice lightly in butter or margarine and place in a 2-quart casserole. Stir in curry powder and onion. Pour on boiling water. Bake, covered, 30–35 minutes, or until rice feels tender when pressed between your fingers and all water is absorbed. Fluff up rice with fork; keep warm until served. Spoon chutney over rice for serving. *Serves 2.*

Fruit and Cheese

Fruit and cheese are always the perfect choice for dessert.*

Brandy

Should be served in snifters from the dime store.☮

☮ See note on page 33.

Food Fit for an . . .
Amorous Athlete

This gentleman (and we use the term loosely) used to throw his moldy hip pads on our best horsehair sofa as he lumbered in. Jinx found Red lounging around Kezar Stadium one Saturday afternoon and promptly mesmerized him with what she likes to refer to as her devilishly tilted eyebrows. There were no violets or snow crocuses or thoughtful bottles of wine from this one— only a rather damp kiss on the cheek and a mumbled, "When's chow?" Alas, he was drafted by the Packers and we heard from him no more.

But while he was around and she still thought he was the greatest living specimen, Jinx forgot the Society section and concentrated on Sandy Koufax's strikeout record and Arnie Palmer's⊕ latest chip-shot technique. Suffice to say, this isn't a bad idea if you've got an athlete on your hands. If he discovers that you, too, like sports, he'll hold you in high esteem along with Wilma Rudolph and Gussie Moran.⊕⊖ Be careful, though, for if you feign your interest too avidly, he'll ask you

---

⊕ We'll take Sandy off the mound and replace him with Roger Clemens; Arnie has retired gracefully, to be replaced by Woods and Els.

⊕⊖ Stellar American athletes of decades past. Drop names like Jackie Joyner and Lindsay Davenport, and you'll be current. As an afterthought, why not buy the newest almanac—it'll tell you who's who in the jock world.

what you think of putting the twenty-four-second rule into college basketball. And then where will you be?

He'll fire no questions, though, if you wave this menu under his broken nose. In fact, he'll probably elect you to his own Hall of Fame.

BEEF BURGUNDY FLAMBÉ
OPEN SESAME NOODLES   GREEN SALAD
HEADY PEACHES
BURGUNDY OR GAMAY

Beef Burgundy Flambé

1 pound round steak or sirloin tip
2 slices bacon
1 bay leaf
½ teaspoon salt
½ teaspoon oregano
¼ teaspoon MSG♥
¼ teaspoon ground pepper
¼ cup garlic-flavored wine vinegar
½ cup Burgundy
¼ cup beef consommé

♥ Forget it.

1 tablespoon flour
5–6 tiny white onions, peeled
1 small green pepper, cut in small pieces
½ pound fresh mushrooms, sliced
¾ cup cherry tomatoes, halved
¼ cup brandy

Cut beef into 1½-inch cubes. Fry bacon crisp in mammoth skillet. Remove bacon and drain. Remove all but 2 tablespoons of the fat from the pan. Add beef in small amounts and brown slowly on all sides. Combine bay leaf, salt, oregano, MSG,♥ pepper, wine vinegar, wine, and consommé; pour over beef. Cover and simmer 1 hour or until beef is almost done.† Thicken gravy with flour mixed with a little water. Add onions; cover and cook 10 minutes. Add green pepper and mushrooms; simmer another 5 minutes. Add tomatoes and cook about 5 minutes. Test to see if onions are tender. Ladle into your prettiest serving dish. Warm brandy slightly; pour over beef and touch a long match to it. Carry flaming to the table. *Serves 2* with good leftovers.

♥ No, no!

Open Sesame Noodles

   1 cup noodles, cooked
   3 tablespoons butter
   1 tablespoon dry bread crumbs
   2 tablespoons sesame seeds
   ½ teaspoon MSG♥
   Salt and pepper

Mix all ingredients and serve immediately. *Serves 2.*

Green Salad

Special Salad* without the tomatoes would be a good complement.

Since your guest for the evening is such a he-man, he'll be delighted that you have kept his physical fitness program in mind as you serve him fruit for dessert. . . .

Heady Peaches

   4 halves fresh or canned peaches
   8 tablespoons chopped almonds
   8 tablespoons powdered sugar, divided
   2 teaspoons citron, chopped
   ½ cup sherry

♥ One more time—just say no!

Peel, pit, and halve the peaches (now don't you wish you'd bought them in a can?). Chop the almonds until mealy. Add half the sugar; mix thoroughly. Add citron and blend. Fill cavities of peaches with mixture; place in shallow baking pan and sprinkle with balance of powdered sugar.† Pour in sherry, allowing a little to dribble over cavity and its filling. Bake at 350° F. for about 10 minutes. *Serve warm to a twosome.*

Food Fit for a . . .
Man with a Method

The only actor in our lives actually belonged to Judy, but he was around so much we began to think of Steven as community property. He was a wild-eyed and thick-maned basso profundo, given to reciting "Horatio at the Bridge" in the middle of the San Francisco Public Library, where he knew he had a captive audience. Unfortunately for Steven and for our grocery bill, he was always unemployed, and we were expected to keep our histrionic genius going. Our only regret is that he never did set foot on the boards, for latest word has it that Steven is married and selling insurance in Long Beach.

If you know a young thespian, it goes without saying that he is starving, so have a heart and feed the poor guy. Lee Strasberg⊕ may offer nourishment for the mind and soul, but the body is left woefully unattended.

⊕ Director of the Actor's Studio since 1949, Strasberg coached the Marlon Brando mumble and the De Niro eyebrow lift.

This man loves atmosphere, so load it on thick—a little Beethoven, a volume of Shakespeare opened to Othello's handkerchief scene tossed casually on the coffee table, and a few old playbills placed effectively about the room should turn the trick.

Wear your cleanest leotards, call him "dahling," and feed him Voluptuous Veal Scaloppine. Wethinks he won't protesteth too much.

VOLUPTUOUS VEAL SCALOPPINE

NOEL'S NOODLES   GREEN SALAD

LEMON SHERBET

CABERNET SAUVIGNON

Voluptuous Veal Scaloppine

1½ pounds veal scaloppine (ask the butcher to cut it for you)
Flour
Salt
Pepper
Paprika
Parmesan cheese
½ pound fresh mushrooms, thinly sliced
4 tablespoons hot butter
1 bouillon cube dissolved in ½ cup boiling water♥
3 tablespoons Marsala wine or sherry

♥ See note on page 85.

Pound the thinly sliced veal with a mallet or have the butcher do it for you. Dredge with flour seasoned with salt, pepper, paprika, and Parmesan cheese. Sauté meat and mushrooms in butter until meat is golden brown on both sides. Remove to hot platter. Add bouillon♥ to pan and stir in wine while scraping the pan well. Pour the sauce over the meat and *serve to 2*.

Noel's Noodles

½ head cabbage, shredded
¼ cup butter, melted
1 teaspoon sugar
Dashes salt and cracked pepper
½ package thin egg noodles, cooked (about 1 cup)

Sauté the cabbage in the butter until lightly browned. Add sugar, salt, and pepper. Add cooked drained noodles and simmer on low flame until hot. *Serves 2*.

Green Salad

Try Green Salad Marinara.*

♥ Broth!

Food Fit for an . . .

Old Charlie

We can't deny it. Everyone has an old Charlie in her life, hidden somewhere among the old pom-poms and discarded sneakers, and we're no different. Ours wasn't any matinee idol and was slightly ubiquitous, but at least we never had to grind a little Cuban heel into his unsuspecting metatarsal to let him know that it was time for him to shuffle off into the evening.

If yours is any kin to Charlie, ten to one has it that he ties his own trout flies, is a whiz at Monopoly, and is sincerely nice to your mother. A rare find, Charlie was so comfortable that we never hesitated to ask him to drop our dirty laundry off at Ho Chow's. He was the guileless type that innocently strolled around on Sunday afternoon at 5 when our hair was in rollers and the stockings were hung on the shower rods with care. Charlie would share Shrimp Wiggle with us and praise us so ecstatically that we almost felt that we had cleared up another social obligation.

Not quite. Once in a while you, too, will become struck with remorse and go to a little effort for your old Charlie. He rates simple fare, because he's the one you'll probably end up marrying; and after all, you don't want to spoil him. The hidden bonus here is that the leftovers make marvelous sandwiches all week long, so you needn't feel that the extra groceries are a total loss.

BURGUNDY MEAT LOAF
CHINESE PEA PODS   OBESE TOMATOES
PARFAIT PIE
MOUNTAIN RED BURGUNDY

Burgundy Meat Loaf

2 pounds ground round
1½ cups uncooked oatmeal
1 cup Burgundy
6 tablespoons chopped onions
1½ tablespoons salt
½ teaspoon pepper
2 eggs, slightly beaten
Generous pinches rosemary, thyme, and oregano

Combine all ingredients and shape in a well-greased loaf pan.†
Bake at 350° F. for 1 hour. *Serves 2* with some left for hearty
sandwiches.

Chinese Pea Pods

Chinese pea pods are crispy tender little unborn peas still in
their pods. They come frozen♀ just like other legumes, and the
directions are on the package. Great! *Serves 2*.

♀ Fresh are easy to find and easier to prepare. Pull off those feisty
strings and sauté in olive oil until just tender, 2–3 minutes.

Obese Tomatoes

2 big fat tomatoes
1 big fat Spanish onion
¼ cup wine vinegar
3 teaspoons sugar
3 teaspoons basil
1 teaspoon tarragon
1 pinch oregano
Salt and pepper to taste
¼ cup olive oil

Slice your big fat tomatoes and cover with a layer of sliced onion. In a separate bowl, combine the vinegar, sugar, and seasonings; then mix the olive oil in well to make a smooth dressing. Now drizzle 1–2 tablespoons of this magic concoction over the sliced onions and tomatoes. Start all over again with the remaining tomatoes, onions, and dressing, and keep repeating until you run out. Refrigerate before serving. *Serves 2.*

Parfait Pie

CRUMB CRUST:
1½ cups fine crumbs (vanilla wafers, graham crackers, stale
 cookies)
½ cup melted butter
¼ cup sugar

Mix all ingredients until sort of spongy but not gluey. Line a 9-inch pie pan with crumb mixture and chill for a couple of hours.

PARFAIT FILLING:
1 package strawberry-flavored Jell-O⸙
1¼ cups boiling water
1 pint vanilla ice cream, slightly soft
1 cup fresh strawberries, cleaned and sweetened

Dissolve Jell-O in water and stir in ice cream until melted. Pour into crust and chill until very, very firm. Garnish with berries. This is ridiculously easy and looks very pretty. If you're feeling courageous, try new combinations of lime Jell-O and crushed pineapple or raspberry Jell-O with fresh raspberries—the possibilities are unlimited. *Serves 6–8.*

⸙ Oh, dear. Did we ever really make this? Anyway, make that the small package of Jell-O.

5

Pandora's Box

This is a private chapter. As Pandora discovered, there are some things best left under cover, and it seems that one of the most closely guarded secrets of the single girl is that she can out-eat any man. We don't want it to be said that we unleashed the furies, so please don't divulge the clandestine contents of this chapter to anyone outside the fold. Unfortunately, the strange mores of our society dictate that a male may snarl and slaver over his food and come back for thirds, but let a hungry girl pick up her fork with a little honest gusto and it's "My, but aren't we putting on a little weight?"

There are two ways around all this hokum: you may lock yourself in the loo with an entire cheesecake some afternoon and turn into a quietly munching glutton for one ecstatic hour, or you can break down and have the girls to dinner. Together you may rid yourselves of frustrations and oral complexes, break all social barriers, and simply *eat*. None of this folderol of picking and shoving your food around your plate—just a good healthy stampede to the table and a riotous grab to see who can get the most food.

If you don't believe us, think back to your dewy-eyed days as a schoolgirl. We used to stand outside the dining room yelling, "Hungerr!" And could we pack away the groceries! We once roomed with a veritable St. Bernard of a girl who invariably knocked down our sweet little housemother, Mrs. Tippytoe, every Wednesday, which was always macaroni and cheese day. Respect for our elders prevents us from mentioning how many girls Mrs. T. could knock down on *her* way to the table.

The glorious thing about feeding and watering females is that you don't have to be the least bit exotic about the whole affair. Remember that they're tired of being coy and sophisticated about eating—all they want is food and plenty of it. Make your menu simple and filling; we found that almost any kind of Italian food is marvelous, for you can make it before the party and it makes up well in enormous batches to allow for seconds and thirds. Plan on an unbelievable amount of food and then plan on a little more. Just to loosen all those inhibitions and pent-up hunger drives, you might offer them a quick belt out of your gin bottle. Or fill your bathtub with Chianti?—it's beautifully cheap and does the trick!

Beware the female! Though she won't be fussy about your cooking, she'll have eyes like Captain Marvel when it comes to spotting that little blob of old toothpaste in your sink or the egg on the salad fork. If you do nothing else, get that apartment clean. They'll talk about the dust curls under your couch long after they've forgotten your heavenly minestrone. The shrews are like that.

At this time in your life, you're going to find that your friends will begin to desert you and do inexplicable things like get married and have babies, and you are going to have to give a shower for at least one of these seemingly misguided souls. We say

---

? All that sounds devil-may-care, but you'd care a whole lot if you had to (1) pay for a bathtub of even the cheapest Chianti and, worse, (2) scrub the rosy thing the next day. Bad idea.

"seemingly" because someday you'll be the burbling center of attention at one of these gatherings, and we guarantee that you, too, will coo ecstatically over spatulas and tea cozies. But if you're still playing the role of hostess, take heart—use the opportunity for a gangfest and you won't have to fool with those fussy shower-type desserts.

The next time some frilly little skirt minces around and tells you she eats like a bird, smile knowingly and invite her up for:

BEER HALL PIE
CHÂTEAU SALAD
VANILLA ICE CREAM WITH COGNAC
COOKIES

Beer Hall Pie

1 cup prepared biscuit mix
⅓ cup milk
1 tablespoon oil⁰
1 pound ground round
1 large onion, sliced thin
1 teaspoon salt
¼ teaspoon pepper
3 tablespoons ketchup
2 tablespoons biscuit mix

⁰ Canola will be just fine here.

2 *eggs, slightly beaten*
1 *cup cottage cheese*
Paprika
Parsley

Combine prepared biscuit mix and milk; muddle the mixture gently around a lightly floured board. Roll it to fit a 9-inch pie pan. Grease pan and fit in dough as you would a piecrust. Heat oil in a skillet; sauté beef and onion until beef is brown and onion is tender. Stir in salt, pepper, ketchup, and the 2 table-spoons biscuit mix. Fill dough shell with meat mixture. Blend eggs with cottage cheese and pour over meat and onion. Bake at 350° F. for 30 minutes. Sprinkle with paprika and garnish with parsley. *Serves 4–6 hungry girls once around.*

Château Salad

1 *small head Bibb lettuce*
1 *head romaine lettuce*
⅓ *cup olive oil*
3 *tablespoons garlic wine vinegar*
2 *teaspoons chervil*
2 *teaspoons Beau Monde*
½ *teaspoon onion salt*
1 *teaspoon mixed salad herbs (available at most large markets)*

Tear greens into bite-size pieces. Mix all other ingredients in a jar; shake well and pour over greens when ready to serve. Toss gently. *Serves 6.*

Vanilla Ice Cream with Cognac

Buy 1 quart of vanilla ice cream for every 4–6 guests. Pour a small amount of cognac over vanilla ice cream in blender or mixing bowl. Break up into small chunks and blend at low speed. Keep adding cognac and blending until ice cream reaches the consistency of cake batter. Serve with crunchy cookies from the bakery. (This is also a goody for ladylike showers.)

We went to great lengths to try to steal a minestrone recipe from Judy's mother, who is famous for her thick Italian soup; but she took to locking her doors at night, so you'll have to be content with our own, which we very immodestly think is pretty good, too. . . .

MINESTRONE
BREAD STICKS   MARINATED VEGETABLES
MISS PIGGY'S DELIGHT

Minestrone

Meaty soup bones (smile at the butcher)
2 quarts water
1 cup chopped celery
1 cup chopped onion
2 bay leaves
Salt and pepper to taste
2 cloves garlic, pressed
2 tablespoons Italian seasoning

1 can (8½ ounces) kidney beans
1 cup chopped cabbage
1 cup diced tomatoes
1 cup zucchini, sliced thin
¼ cup chopped parsley
8 ounces spaghetti, macaroni, or favorite pasta

Brown soup bones in a 350° F. oven for about 35 minutes. Place in your biggest kettle and add water, celery, onion, bay leaves, salt, pepper, garlic, and Italian seasoning. (If your grocer is backward and doesn't carry Italian seasoning, try a fat pinch each of marjoram, oregano, rosemary, and basil.) Cover and simmer for 2–3 hours; cool and skim off fat that—if it is any kind of self-respecting fat—has risen to the top. Add beans, cabbage, tomatoes, zucchini, and parsley,♥ and simmer for another hour or until vegetables are tender.† Add spaghetti, simmer 30 minutes, and serve piping hot in preheated bowls. *Serves 6 generously.*

♥ Since we've now learned it's better not to cook vegetables until they shout "Uncle," we suggest that you add the beans and cabbage, cook for an hour, but keep the tomatoes and zucchini out of the pot until about 10 minutes before the soup is done, and add the parsley just before serving.

Marinated Vegetables

2 dozen cherry tomatoes
2 jars (6 ounces each) marinated artichoke hearts
2 Bermuda onions, sliced
3 cucumbers, sliced

Arrange all ingredients on a tray or platter, and drizzle the tangiest dressing you can find over the whole affair. Refrigerate until ready to serve, then place the tray in the center of your table as an attractive—and highly edible—centerpiece. *Serves 6.*

Miss Piggy's Delight☺

1 pint heavy whipping cream, chilled
½ cup powdered sugar
3 tablespoons instant coffee powder
Pinch salt
1 teaspoon vanilla

☺ The divine Miss Piggy had not yet hoofed her way into our hearts when this recipe made its first appearance. Now that she has, we can appropriately name this gooey delight for one of our favorite divas. Go ahead, pig out!

1 *envelope unflavored gelatin*
¼ *cup cold water*
9-*inch baked pastry shell*

Combine cream, sugar, coffee powder, salt, and vanilla in a bowl. Soften gelatin in cold water in a saucepan, then heat until gelatin is thoroughly dissolved. Remove from heat. Gradually pour gelatin into cream mixture, and beat until blended thoroughly. Pour into shell and chill for at least 1 hour. Garnish with shaved chocolate and chopped nuts. *Serves 6–8.*

This next menu is centered around rigatoni, a not-too-hackneyed Italian pasta that is embarrassingly cheap and delightfully filling. But heed. Never attempt to prepare this wonderful dish for more than 6 unless you have legs of iron and nerves of steel. Stuffing the rigatoni takes considerable time and is truly an idiot's delight. Try it anyway. It's worth it.

RIGATONI
BROCCOLI VINAIGRETTE
CRUSTY FRENCH BREAD
BAKED GRAPEFRUIT

Rigatoni

1½ *pounds mixed ground round, veal, and pork*
¼ *cup chopped onion*
4 *cans (8 ounces each) tomato sauce*

1 can (3 ounces) tomato paste
2 tablespoons Italian seasoning
Salt and pepper to taste
1 pound rigatoni shells
½ cup cooked chopped spinach
¼ cup Parmesan cheese, grated
1 large garlic clove, pressed
1 egg
1 teaspoon salt
½ teaspoon pepper

Get out your skillet and first make a tomato sauce by sautéing ½ pound of the mixed ground meat with the chopped onion until the meat is brown and the onion tender. Add tomato sauce, tomato paste, Italian seasoning, and salt and pepper to taste; simmer for 30 minutes, stirring occasionally. Pour half of this tomato sauce in the bottom of a buttered baking dish.

Boil the rigatoni shells according to directions on the package. While that's bubbling away, combine in a bowl the remaining pound of raw meat and the spinach, cheese, garlic, egg, salt, and pepper, and mix well. Drain and rinse the rigatoni shells in a colander under running water. Now! Stuff each and every little shell with the raw meat–spinach mixture and place on top of the tomato sauce.❦ Pour remaining tomato sauce over the rigatoni shells, sprinkle with more Parmesan, and bake for 35 minutes uncovered in a 350° F. oven. If you'd like to make this ahead of time, make it the day before: bake for 20 minutes at 350° and refrigerate.† Reheat for 15 minutes at 350°, *cover,* and heat for 20 more minutes at 350°. *Serve bubbling hot to* 6 hungry ladies.

> ♀ Let's say you've just had a manicure. Or let's say that you simply don't fancy spending half a day stuffing little pasta tubes. Well, then, do what any sane person would do and layer the tomato sauce, the pasta, the meat and spinach mixture, and the remaining tomato sauce and pop it in the oven. There. That's done.

Broccoli Vinaigrette

2 packages frozen broccoli spears♀♀
Lettuce leaves
Olive oil
Lemon juice
Fat pinch each minced parsley, chives, salt, and tarragon

Cook broccoli according to package directions; drain and chill. Arrange chilled spears on lettuce leaves. Combine equal parts olive oil and lemon juice in a jar; add remaining ingredients, and shake well. Pour over broccoli. *Serves 6.*

♀♀ Steam fresh stalks for 5–6 minutes, or use our favorite green vegetable trick: Prep and put in a sealable plastic bag with a tablespoon of water. Nuke for 2 minutes. Crispy, green, and crunchy, with virgin vitamins intact.

Baked Grapefruit

½ grapefruit per person
Cinnamon candies
Sherry
Brown sugar

Section each grapefruit half carefully. Fill center cavity with small red cinnamon candies, and ladle 1 tablespoon sherry over the meat of the fruit. Sprinkle with brown sugar until the fruit will absorb no more.† Bake in a 350° F. oven about 20 minutes. Prepare 4–5 hours ahead of time; the cinnamon candies will turn the grapefruit pink, and your friends will think you spent a fortune.

Baffled we are. Just what *can* we say about spaghetti that is *très gai* and a million laughs? Very little, of course. But we can remind you that everybody loves it, and it's so cheap that the money you have saved will add another share of IBM to your portfolio—well, almost.

SPAGHETTI
ANTIPASTO SALAD
EUROPEAN BREADBASKET
SHERBET SARAH BERNHARDTS
CHIANTI

Spaghetti

3 slices bacon, minced
¼ cup chopped onion
2 cloves garlic, pressed
1 pound ground round
2½ cups solid-pack tomatoes with juice
½ cup chopped green pepper
½ pound sliced fresh mushrooms, sautéed
Salt and pepper to taste
1 can (3 ounces) tomato paste
1 bay leaf
Fat pinches each oregano, rosemary, and basil
1 pound spaghetti

Cook bacon slowly over a low flame; stir in onion, garlic, and ground round. Sauté until tender and brown; add tomatoes, green pepper, mushrooms, salt, pepper, tomato paste, bay leaf, and seasonings; simmer for at least 1 hour (the longer, the better). If you are of our spaghetti school and like the sauce and the pasta all muddled together, you can cook the spaghetti now, stir in the sauce, and refrigerate.† Reheat, covered, at 350° F. for

35–40 minutes. However, if you're a direct descendant of da Vinci, you probably will want to serve it the die-hard Italian way with the sauce poured over the naked pasta. This is fine—it simply means that you'll have to reheat the sauce when you cook the pasta at the last minute. It's a lot more bothersome work and who needs it? By the way, add olive oil and salt to the water when cooking the spaghetti, and cook *just* until tender, about 8–10 minutes. *Serves 6.*

Antipasto Salad

1 *head iceberg lettuce, torn*
¼ *cup salami, cut in small pieces*
¼ *pound Monterey Jack or provolone cheese, cut in small pieces*
2 *tablespoons capers*
¼ *cup pepperoncini (optional)*
Dehydrated Italian dressing, prepared according to directions on
    package⸔

To greens, add salami, cheese, capers, and pepperoncini; toss with your favorite packaged Italian dressing. *Serves 6.*

European Breadbasket

If you're fortunate enough to live in a fairly cosmopolitan city, finding a delicatessen or a bakery that produces fresh European breads will be no problem. Buy an imaginative assortment and

---

⸔ See note on page 189.

nestle them in a basket lined with a red and white checked napkin or bandana, from Mr. Woolworth's general store.

Sherbet

Most cities have a mammoth ice-cream emporium that boasts 3,003 flavors or some such nonsense. At any rate, there are probably quite a few, and among them you can find a tart and refreshing sherbet such as daiquiri ice or pink grapefruit ice to serve after this heavy meal. With it you can serve:

Sarah Bernhardts⊕

4 cups old-fashioned oatmeal
2 cups brown sugar
½ pound butter or margarine, melted
2 tablespoons vanilla

Mix all ingredients and fill muffin tins half full. Bake at 350° F. for about 15 minutes. Cool for 15 more minutes and remove from tins. *Makes 2 dozen* dangerous cookies.

Or as a last ditch, you might try:

⊕ A world-famous turn-of-the-century diva.

Pizza
Green Salad Marinara
Beer

All growing girls love pizza and beer, but as you may have discovered, homemade pizza just hasn't got it. Besides, we don't have a recipe. Why not let Little Joe or Rudolfo or Georgino or whatever your little old pizza-maker calls himself whip up an assortment of juicy pizzas, to be picked up by you right before the party and whisked into the oven and kept warm until serving time? Serve with huge schooners of beer and:

Green Salad Marinara

1½ heads romaine lettuce
Dehydrated Italian dressing, prepared according to directions on packageᵈ
1 small can anchovy fillets
1 cup garlic-flavored croutons

Tear greens into bite-size pieces. Add drained anchovy fillets to greens, along with croutons. Pour dressing over salad and toss. *Serves 6.*

You probably won't want dessert, as most young ladies seem to eat pizza to a point of no return; but if you feel you must, try the light sherbet or ice routine again.

ᵈ Try dressing for Special Salad, p. 88.

SHOWERS

Let us return to showers briefly. If you shun the idea of concocting an entire dinner before the opening of all the little gifty-nifty items, you may fall back upon the ladylike type of shower that includes only dessert. Being an independent career girl possessing a wealth of savoir faire, you probably have a very dim view of girlish doings. Nevertheless, if you'll let down the blasé bit for just an evening, we think you'll discover they're really not so bad.

The biggest headache involved is the problem of what kind of shower to give. Your best bet is to ask the guest of honor if she has any preference; perhaps she has twelve full sets of towels and sheets and nary an egg timer. However, if she doesn't speak up bravely for the old kitchen and linen standbys, why not plan a shower around one of the following:

Paper: In addition to the usual kitchen wraps, books, and magazine subscriptions, think of gift-wrap assortments, tickets to a hit show, a lovely pen-and-ink drawing, or even honeymoon tickets or a check—from parents, of course.

Cookbooks: Make sure she really *likes* to cook. Only a lover of food and kitchens truly appreciates cookbooks. Compare notes beforehand to guard against duplicates.

Sewing: Again, make sure of her interest. You, as a hostess, give the sewing basket, and each guest brings a specific sewing article. Your guest of honor unwraps the sewing basket first and then proceeds to fill it with each gift as she unwraps.

Spice Shelf: As hostess, you give her the spice shelf, and each guest brings a jar of predesignated spice (all from the same manufacturer, for appearance's sake) and a recipe calling for that spice.

Dining Room: All the things to make a table prettier—candles, mats, napkins, napkin rings, clever decorations for different seasons, unusual serving dishes, candlesticks, place-card holders. . . .

Boudoir: Anything lovely for the bride's closet and bath. A myriad of possibilities here, from bath oil to scales to padded hangers.

Recipe Shower: Each guest brings not only a recipe, but the pot in which it should be cooked.

Now for the little headache: what to serve for a ladylike dessert. Any of the following suggestions are regrettably simple and ultrafeminine:

- If you have a large glass salad bowl, fill it with scoops of assorted pastel sherbets and ices. That 3,003 flavors place will usually make up the assortment for you so that you aren't eating leftover pistachio nut for the rest of your life. It makes an unusually pretty dessert, and this way each guest can probably find a flavor she likes; if she can't, ask her to leave quietly.

- Drizzle Kahlua over coffee ice cream and serve with crunchy cookies.
- Or why not steaming cups of coffee and assorted French pastries from the best bakery in town?
- Or Irish coffee?

But if you feel your reputation is at stake and you must go to some effort, you can make this a week ahead of time—and it *is* impressive:

Gooey Baked Alaska

(Men have died for it)

2 pints coffee or strawberry ice cream
1 package brownie mix
5 egg whites
12 tablespoons granulated sugar

While you're letting the ice cream soften, prepare brownie mix according to directions. Bake in an 8-inch round pan and cool. Line a 7- to 8-inch bowl with waxed paper and pour in the softened ice cream; freeze until solid. When ice cream is frozen and brownie is completely cool, beat the egg whites at high speed until foamy. Add the sugar gradually and beat until meringue holds stiff peaks. Set aside. Transfer brownie to small board or any flat, metal sheet that can go from freezer to oven. Invert bowl of ice cream over brownie and peel off paper. Spread meringue over the ice cream dome and freeze℗ until just before serving time.† Bake at 500° F. for 2 minutes or until meringue is lightly browned. If you wish to transfer to a pretty serving plate, now is the time. Let stand for 10 or more minutes, until you can cut it easily. *Serves 8–10.*

℗ It's quite simple: meringue will not endure freezing and thawing. One could liken it to a virtual reality of the demise of the *Titanic*—broken, sodden, tragic. Our suggestion is to execute the brownie/ice cream gambit and wrap it well for the freezer. When it's time to serve, make the meringue, cloak the lovely dome, and continue with the instructions for baking at 500°. Let stand for ice cream to soften. There!

6

Deadly Little Dinners

You think the title is funny? You won't.

There will come a time, most assuredly, when sweet lavender-and-old-lace relatives will descend upon you and plop themselves and their silk jersey prints smack into the middle of your usually euphoric state. By all means, hide the gin, slip into your ruffled gingham, and strew your old merit badges from Troop 63 about conspicuously.

This is definitely not the time for a juicy Crabmeat Flambé or a lovely bottle of Riesling; remember the impression you are trying to create with these dear old souls who are categorically suspicious of Youth and the Big City. You must send them on their way, once again assured that you are the same sweet Susie. They must feel that your day starts off with a steamy cup of hot chocolate and a wave at the friendly corner policeman, that you spend all of your evenings washing either your hair or your underwear. Never, never let on that you like martinis, sports cars, and James Baldwin novels or send your laundry out. It's all right to mention old Charlie and his trout flies, but never the young man from BBD&O, for he must surely be a Dreiserian masher.

There are only three menus included here, but after all, let's hope you won't have to do this too often. We've called them Deadly because that's just what these little dinners are. Make them hefty, starchy, and filling meals designed to reassure the folks back in Ohio that you've got your brogans planted firmly on the ground. However, we found that adults have a mysterious way of becoming human somewhere about the time you reach your twenty-first birthday. It's amazing how much wiser they get, so it might be a good idea to have a substantial bottle of wine stashed away just in case they turn out to be swingers.⊕

There is a funny fine line that must be drawn between parents and older relatives. Parents should be handled deftly; you want to impress them with your newfound prowess as a cook and the maturity with which you have met your new situation in life. Yet they must feel that you are still unabashedly Their Little Girl.

When considering parents as dinner guests, you must be the one to decide just how much exotic food and drink they'll stand for. If you're not sure, take the cautious route—whip up a Deadly Little Dinner, but embellish or revise it as you see fit. Reassure them with pot roast, but hint at your maturity by opening a fine Cabernet and sniffing the bouquet knowledgeably. They're not apt to think you've turned wino at twenty-two.

There is one unusual candidate for a Deadly Little Dinner: that nice boy who fixed your car last week. You probably don't want to encourage him, for the type that willingly fixes cars has got to be a strange breed, but you do owe him something. Feed him Onion-Glazed Pork Chops and Potatoes au Gratin, and he'll never come back. But then, he's probably such a clod that he will. Ah, well, that's your problem and not ours—you could have burned them, you know.

⊕ My, doesn't the vernacular evolve? Swingers used to be just nice folks who liked to party once in a while. Today, well . . . let's not go there.

Deadly Little Dinner #1

ONION-GLAZED PORK CHOPS
GREEN BEANS AMANDINE
POTATOES AU GRATIN
APPLE PIE
COFFEE   TEA

Onion-Glazed Pork Chops

1 package dried onion soup mix ℓ
2 cups water
6 pork chops, 1 inch thick

Combine the soup mix and water and simmer for 5 minutes. Arrange pork chops in a single layer in a large, shallow baking dish. Ladle onion soup over the chops. Bake uncovered at 350° F. for 1½ hours, ℓℓ or until tender and glazed. *Serves 3.*

ℓ There was a time when dried onion soup mix was every busy cook's best friend. Few would admit to using it today, but you may be surprised by how easy and tasty this way with a pork chop is. We suggest, however, that you dispose of any traces of the dried soup envelope before guests arrive.

♫ Years ago, pork was always incinerated because people feared trichinosis. Today we know that trichinae are destroyed at a temperature of 137°, but that is still really too pink for most people. These chops will be tender and still moist if you bake them for only about 45 minutes or until they register about 160° on an instant-read meat thermometer. Now we cover the baking dish with foil for the first 30 minutes or so to help keep the pork moist. Live and learn.

Green Beans Amandine

While you're melting down a package of frozen French-cut string beans, sauté a small fistful of slivered almonds in butter. When beans are tender but still slightly crisp, drain, then add almonds, butter, and 1 tablespoon lemon juice. Toss lightly. *Serves 3*.

Potatoes au Gratin

Take a package off the shelf and prepare according to directions.

Apple Pie

We'll never tell if you take it out of the freezer and follow directions.

This next one's really rather good, so don't waste it on just anybody. It's worthy of parents, for it takes some effort on your part, and they'll be twice as appreciative as you ever were for your college education. If you'd like to dress it up, import a fancy dessert from the bakery in place of the vanilla ice cream and demitasse, which is strictly for Little Old Ladies from Pasadena.

Deadly Little Dinner #2

HERBED ROAST LEG OF LAMB
CAULIFLOWER WITH NEW PEAS
AND HOLLANDAISE
MINT SAUCE
VANILLA ICE CREAM
DEMITASSE

Herbed Roast Leg of Lamb

1 6-pound leg of lamb
1 garlic clove, crushed
1½ teaspoons salt
1 teaspoon freshly ground pepper
2 tablespoons olive oil
1 teaspoon marjoram
1 teaspoon rosemary
1 teaspoon thyme
2 tablespoons flour
1 cup dry white wine
1 cup water

Place lamb in a shallow roasting pan without a rack. Crush garlic in a small bowl with salt and pepper. Mix with olive oil and rub on lamb with fingers. Sprinkle roast with marjoram, rosemary, thyme, and flour. Pour wine and water in pan with lamb (not *on* lamb). Roast at 325° F. for 2½–3 hours or to internal temperature of 140°, basting every 25–30 minutes. *Serves 6.*

Cauliflower with New Peas and Hollandaise

Prepare a whole cauliflower the way your doorstopper cookbook tells you to, and melt down 1½–2 packages of petite peas or regular peas if you can't sleuth down the others. Place the whole cauliflower on a large serving platter, surrounded with peas, and pour heated canned hollandaise sauce*ℓ* over all. *Serve at once to 6 people.*

ℓ We're not too sure that this product still exists, and since it's so easy to whip up hollandaise in a blender, why bother to look for it? To make a quick hollandaise sauce, put 2 egg yolks in a blender or food processor, whirl, and gradually add 1½ tablespoons boiling water very slowly. Whirl it a bit more and then slowly add ½ pound melted hot butter in a thin stream. Add 1 tablespoon lemon juice, a dash of cayenne pepper, and salt to taste. This makes about 1¼ cups. We thank Marion Cunningham for revising the old *Fannie Farmer Cookbook* and giving us this recipe, which we've used for years.

Mint Sauce

The mint sauce or mint-flavored apple jelly can be found in the gourmet section of the supermarket. At least we hope it can, for we haven't the foggiest notion of how it's made.

This last one's a real winner. It's so wholesome that it fairly screams of orthopedic oxfords and dimity camisoles. Nevertheless, it tastes good, and the leftovers make their own stew.

Deadly Little Dinner #3

YANKEE POT ROAST WITH NOODLES
YOUNG PEAS
SWEET CARROTS
POUND CAKE   COFFEE

Yankee Pot Roast with Noodles

You're in luck if you have a fairly deep (3-inch) electric frying pan. Otherwise, use a Dutch oven.♥ If you have neither, forget it and go back to Onion-Glazed Pork Chops.

♥ This cooking gear may not be in your personal kitchen collection, but all you need is a heavy covered casserole or pot that can be used on top of the stove and then transferred to the oven. Just remember to check the handles for being ovenproof, lest you have a forced encounter with your local fireman.

3 tablespoons flour
1½ teaspoons salt
½ teaspoon pepper
3–4 pounds beef chuck, 3 inches thick
3 tablespoons fat𝒹
¾ cup boiling water
1 can (12 ounces) solid-pack tomatoes
¼ cup coarsely chopped celery
¼ cup sliced onion

Combine flour, salt, and pepper and dredge the beef in this mixture. Set frying pan at 375° F.; add fat. When fat is very hot, brown the meat on both sides and spoon off the excess fat. Reduce temperature to 210°. Add remaining ingredients and cover. Cook for at least 3 hours or until tender. Add more water as needed. *Serves 4* with plenty of leftovers.

While you're cooking the Noodles in boiling salted water, melt down the Young Peas from a frozen package, and open a couple of cans of those Sweet Baby Carrots𝒱 and heat.

𝒹 Opt for some quality olive oil here.

𝒱 Frozen peas, especially *petit pois*, are quite all right. But find some baby carrots in the produce section, scrape them nicely, and steam them until tender. Those prebagged carrots that look like little orange torpedoes taste of chemicals and plastic.

Pound Cake

Pound cake is a favorite with the elderly set, though slightly reminiscent of asbestos. Slice a frozen pound cake into thin pieces and camouflage with some heated caramel sauce and toasted slivered almonds if you like.

All this has been a grim prospect for a chill winter's eve when you could have been tucked cosily in Sardi's with some handsome, heartless dog, but we thought we ought to warn you, for at some time in your gay young life, it will happen to you. Be a good sport and make the best of it—tomorrow night you can pamper yourself with Oysters Rockefeller and a heavenly Pot de Crème.

7

Beautiful Brunches

During our neophyte career-girl era, we discovered one of the great unsung means of entertaining—the brunch. Brunches are just chock-full of good qualities, not the least of which is that they are cheaper than a full-fledged dinner. It's a rare guest who expects a filet mignon or a ten-rib roast of beef at 11 in the morning. In addition, brunches are less work than any other meal for which you might be tempted to call a gathering of the clan. There is also the obvious advantage that no one is really awake and so they won't be too critical of your culinary efforts.

However, even brunches have their drawbacks. Since you will probably be just as droopy-eyed as your guests, you'd better have everything as carefully calculated as the Normandy invasion. No last-minute trips to the corner shop for the neglected carton of eggs, please.

The night before, you can set the table, sweep the rug, and remove any large objects of clutter such as that pile of clothes for the Goodwill that has been heaped peacefully in the middle of the living room for the past month. Don't leave it there till morning or you will trip complacently over it in your fuzzy little scuffs and never even know it's there.

Probably the worst thing about brunches is getting up out of your nice woolly bed to face your stove at an hour when it will seem even more formidable than usual. But set yourself on automatic pilot and get busy. You'll be surprised by what you can accomplish on only two cylinders, and as we said, your guests won't be in any condition to criticize.

When the doorbell rings and you drift hazily toward it, don't be surprised to be greeted by a band of disgustingly jolly and hungry people. Some people simply are that way in the morning, though they may be perfectly delightful at any other time of the day. Don't blink an eye. Just paste on your very best pompom-girl smile and hand them something large, juicy, and faintly alcoholic. If that doesn't settle them down, just remember never to invite them back for anything earlier than a midnight supper.

Now you can, in all good conscience, waft gently back to the kitchen and gulp down a steaming cup of coffee while you finish whipping up:

SOUSED MELON

EGGS VALENTINE

ENGLISH MUFFINS

STRAWBERRY JAM   ORANGE MARMALADE

COFFEE

Soused Melon

Buy a lovely honeydew if it's in season (ask that nice motherly lady pushing her cart around the produce section to find a ripe one for you) or two boxes of frozen melon balls.❓ Divide into

---

❓ An unsuspecting melon will suffer an untimely demise when exposed to freezing temperatures. Let your greengrocer pick out a healthy melon for you, and scoop it out with your handy melon baller (which we should have mentioned in chapter 1—sorry about that).

6 fairly equal portions, which you will place comfortably in a dish and lace heartily with good Port wine.

Eggs Valentine

1½ pounds crabmeat
3 cans cream sauce?
Salt and pepper
6 eggs
Swiss cheese, grated
Butter

Mix crabmeat with cream sauce. Toss in a healthy dash of salt and pepper. Put 1 spoonful in the bottom of each of six buttered ramekins (a ramekin, *mon enfant*, is a tiny ovenproof dish). Break an egg on top of each spoonful. Salt and pepper eggs, add a little more crabmeat and cream sauce on top, sprinkle with grated Swiss cheese and bits of butter, and bake at 350° F. for 15–19 minutes. If you don't happen to have six little ramekins reposing smugly on your cupboard shelf, you can do it in your brave old casserole dish. *Serves 6*.

? There's that pesky cream sauce again. See note on page 14.

JUICED ORANGE JUICE
OR
SCREWDRIVERS
EGGS IN THEIR CUPS
BACON
BREAKFAST ROLLS
COFFEE

Juiced Orange Juice

Make up 2 cans of frozen orange juice.♥ For each guest, beat
1 cup chilled orange juice into 1 lightly beaten egg, and add
1 ounce sherry.

Screwdrivers

For each serving, put 2–3 ice cubes into a tall glass. Add 2 ounces
vodka and fill the rest of the glass with orange juice.

♥ Now that we have delicious fresh orange juice in cartons, why not
use that instead? Suit yourself and choose the juice with no pulp,
some pulp, or enough pulp to make Presto logs. We don't care.

Eggs in Their Cups

3 large tomatoes
6 eggs
Butter
¼ teaspoon salt
Dash fresh-cracked Java black pepper
2 cans cream sauce?
1 can mushroom pieces♪
1 tablespoon curry powder
Pinch tarragon

Cut tomatoes in half; remove the pulp and drain. Into each tomato half, break an egg, dot with butter, and sprinkle with salt and pepper. Bake at 350° F. until eggs are firm. While the eggs are baking, heat the cream sauce and add mushrooms, curry powder, and tarragon. When tomato cups are ready, serve with the cream sauce on top. *Serves 6.*

Bacon

Well, your mother did teach you *something*, didn't she?

Breakfast Rolls

Your best bet is to nip on down to your nearest jolly baker for these. Pop them into the oven when you put in the eggs, and they will be warmed through when you're ready for them.

? Did we own stock in some cream sauce company? See note on page 14.
♪ Use one cup fresh sliced mushrooms.

BULLSHOT
PINEAPPLE CHUNKS WITH ORANGE JUICE
FRANÇOIS' FRENCH TOAST
CANADIAN BACON
COFFEE

Bullshot

For each serving, pour 1½ ounces vodka into a short, squat glass. Fill with bouillon. Be sure not to use consommé, as it will jell when cold, and no one should have to face a quivering glass in the morning.

Pineapple Chunks with Orange Juice

For each guest, place ¾ cup chunked pineapple in a dish or wide-mouthed glass, and douse each with ¼ cup orange juice.

François' French Toast

We understand that this was served at the Plaza Hotel⊕ in New York for Sunday breakfast, by a chef named François Gouron.

⊕ In one of the worst development decisions of our time, the Plaza Hotel is now the Plaza Condos or some such. And where, pray tell, is Eloise supposed to live?

But since neither of us has more than a nodding acquaintance with Eloise or Skipperdee, we can't really be sure.

2 eggs
Powdered sugar
2 cups light cream
Pinch salt
½ teaspoon vanilla
⅓ cup rum or brandy
12 slices French bread, cut in thick slices on a slant
Butter
¼ cup applesauce
¾ cup thin custard sauce (see below)

Beat the eggs, 1½ tablespoons powdered sugar, cream, salt, vanilla, and rum or brandy together. Dip the slices of bread in this and sauté in butter until about the shade of Clairol Honey Beige. Arrange the slices of bread in a casserole. Mix the applesauce and custard sauce and pour over the toast. Sprinkle with powdered sugar and bake at 375° F. until brown and bubbly, about 15 minutes. *Serves 6.*

CUSTARD SAUCE:
½ cup milk
1 egg
1 tablespoon granulated sugar
Pinch salt
½ teaspoon vanilla

Heat milk in double boiler until tiny bubbles form. In medium bowl, beat egg slightly with a fork; stir in sugar, salt, and vanilla. Add hot milk slowly, stirring constantly to avoid little cooked egg globs. Return custard to the double boiler and continue cooking until thickened, stirring constantly. *Makes ¾ cup.*

Next time why don't you just get somebody to take you to the Plaza Hotel and let François do all that work?

BLOODY MARYS
FRESH SLICED ORANGES
CURRIED EGGS ON TOASTED
ENGLISH MUFFINS
CANADIAN BACON
COFFEE

Bloody Marys

For each little nodding head, pour 1½ ounces vodka over ice cubes in a tall glass. Fill to the top with vegetable or tomato juice, add ¼ lemon, cracked pepper, dashes of Worcestershire sauce and Tabasco, and ¼ teaspoon of horseradish. Stir well. And blessings on you.

Fresh Sliced Oranges

Peel and slice 1 orange for each guest, sprinkle with sugar, and let stand for about 1 hour before serving.

Curried Eggs on Toasted English Muffins

Halve English muffins, spread with butter, and have ready to slide into broiler. Allow about 1½ muffins per person.

> *12 hard-boiled eggs⊕ (10 minutes)*
> *3 cans white sauce𝒹*
> *½ cup milk*
> *3 teaspoons curry powder*

Start the eggs in cold water and boil about 10 minutes. Hold under running water until cool enough to peel. To the white sauce add milk and curry powder, and heat until smooth and creamy. Slice eggs into cream sauce and heat thoroughly while you're toasting the English muffins and finishing frying the Canadian bacon. A delightful sunny yellow concoction. *Serves* 6 hungry people.

⊕ In foodie circles, one now says "hard-cooked," reserving the term *hard-boiled* for Raymond Chandler–esque detectives.

𝒹 Yikes! See note on page 14.

SALTY DOGS
MUSHROOMS MAGNIFIQUE
CROISSANTS
COFFEE

Salty Dogs

For each guest, wet the rim of a glass with lemon juice; dip in salt. When salt has dried, fill glass with ice cubes. Pour in 2 ounces vodka and fill glass with grapefruit juice.

Mushrooms Magnifique

4 tablespoons butter
1 medium onion, diced fine
1 pound mushrooms, sliced
Salt and pepper to taste
1 teaspoon paprika
1 teaspoon lemon juice
1½ cups sour cream
6 slices grilled ham, about ¼ inch thick, or Canadian bacon
Buttered toast
Minced fresh parsley

Melt butter in large skillet and sauté the onion. Add the mushrooms, which have been washed but not peeled before slic-ing. Sauté until mushrooms are tender but not limp or shriveled. Add salt, pepper, paprika, lemon juice, and sour cream. Heat through very gently but thoroughly. Sour cream must not be allowed to bubble. To serve, place a slice of grilled ham or Canadian bacon on each slice of buttered toast or on toast points attractively arranged. Spoon mushrooms over ham and sprinkle with minced fresh parsley. *Serves 6.*

Croissants

Your jolly old baker probably has these too, but if everyone wants to think you had them jetted directly from the Left Bank, you're not going to disillusion them, are you?

You may have to take to your bed for several days after one of these ambitious projects. But you deserve a short sick leave anyway, and remember that everyone you invited now owes you something—a dinner at the Four Seasons or a trip to Rome or a bottle of Chanel. Now there's something to think about while you're washing those stacks of dishes.

8
Posh Picnics
OR:
Walden Revisited

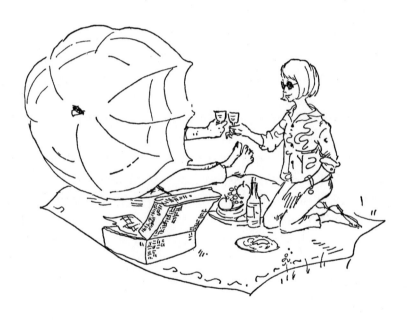

In spring a young girl's fancy lightly turns to thoughts of trips to the Caribbean, racy red sports cars, and posh picnics. Of course, it also turns to thoughts of men—but that's a year-round preoccupation, so it goes without saying. When the first blush of spring fever wafts over you as you sit dreaming at your trusty IBM,⊕ haul out this chapter and begin making plans for a picnic to end all picnics.

You may fade into the carpet at the thought of cold fried chicken packed in old shoe boxes and limp celery sticks made with loving hands by Aunt Sadie the night before that family-reunion picnic. Forget it. That's not what we're talking about. And we're not talking about the impromptu picnic that sounds so mad and young and gay and is usually just a mishmash of old leftovers that aren't fit to serve from a table.

A posh picnic is *strictly for two* and can be a highly romantic little soirée if you have taken the time to make it so. It will involve some gourmet planning and probably some liberal spending, but the rewards will be worth it.

If you haven't a park or a secluded beach or an old mountain lying around, what's wrong with the balcony of your apartment or even the living room floor? Granted you might have to give your roommate a dollar to go to a show, but you can't have everything.

⊕ See history lesson on page 12.

A few notes on sophisticated picnickers:

1. They never, never use paper anythings. Not even napkins.

2. They always take along those little prepackaged washcloths. (Can *you* look seductive with mustard on your nose?)

3. They swear that insulated bags are a must.

4. If they must make it an impromptu affair, they leap over to the deli for navel-busters. Please, no peanut butter and jelly.

5. They always poke holes in watermelons and fill them with rum before going to Jones Beach. Delightful.

6. They feel silly carrying watermelons to football games, so a hip flask of vodka suffices. Make your own Scrooge-drivers with the hawker's orange drink.

After you try the following menus, try devising some of your own. Make it a glamorous affair; fill with succulent foods and a delightful juice of the grape. You may never come home. . . .

Twin Peaks Picnic

COLD LOBSTER

HERB BREAD   TARRAGON BUTTER

CHILLED WHITE WINE

Cold Lobster

If you're brave, throw 2 lobsters (about 1 pound each) into boiling water and turn heat down to a low simmer.🕒 Those little demons will turn red in about 20–25 minutes. Turn off the fire and let cool in the water. Refrigerate until ready to go. Pack in an insulated bag.

Herb Bread

Slice a loaf of French bread, spread with melted butter, sprinkle with thyme, and pop into the oven to warm thoroughly.

Tarragon Butter

Melt 1½ sticks unsalted butter (you'll find it in your supermarket) with 1 teaspoon tarragon. Pack in jar or other glass container.

🕒 The animal-rights folks will tell you that it's cruel to drop lobsters into boiling water, but inasmuch as lobsters have brains the size of your average *petit pois*, we still do it this way, heartless wenches that we are.

Pop the jar of Tarragon Butter into an insulated bag; the wine and the Herb Bread each cuddle in its own insulated bag also. Don't forget nutcrackers or an old screwdriver to pry open the lobster. Take off for parts unknown.

Old Charlie's Picnic

SUBMARINE SANDWICHES
DEVILED EGGS   ICE-COLD BEER

When old Charlie calls to suggest a picnic, the event should be considered as an affliction rather than a soigné tête-à-tête. What he really is asking is that you rustle up some food! Since you wouldn't dream of going to any trouble for your old Charlie, hie yourself to the local supermarket and load up on all the makings for this picnic. Gently pitch 3 eggs into some cold water and bring to a boil.♥ While they're boiling (about 15 minutes),

♥ Over the years, a number of intricate methods for preparing the perfect hard-cooked egg have come and gone. After much trial and error, we've decided we like to gently place the eggs in boiling water, turn the water down to a simmer, and cook them for 10 minutes. Then we pop them into ice water. If all goes well and the moon is in the seventh house, they should have nice yellow yolks with no telltale greenish rings and should peel easily.

assemble long French rolls, salami, cheeses, onion rings, luncheon meats, lettuce, relishes, mayonnaise, mustard, horseradish, tuna, and salad dressing. Build whatever you want when you get to that secluded meadow.

Deviled Eggs

Now halve the eggs, scoop out the yolks, and mash with 2 tablespoons mayonnaise, ½ teaspoon hot prepared mustard, ¼ teaspoon salt, dash pepper, and ½ teaspoon parsley flakes.♪ Stuff back into whites. *Serves 2.*

Stash the beer in a cooler and be on your way.

Thanksgiving Day Picnic

(Why not? You don't know *how* to roast a turkey.)

COLD ROAST CHICKEN
CHILLED ARTICHOKES   LEMON BUTTER
PUMPERNICKEL SANDWICHES
CHILLED WHITE WINE

If you live in the East, you probably won't be going anywhere on Thanksgiving Day, but if the weather is poor, this might be a good chance to try out the living room floor for your picnic.

♪ Take a giant step: use fresh Italian flat-leaf parsley instead. It jumpstarts the taste buds.

A picnic is supposed to be fun for you, too, so why not let the local deli roast that little rooster for you? Cook the artichokes the night before, drain, and chill overnight. Or you can use chilled marinated artichoke hearts. Spread thinly sliced pumpernickel bread with unsalted butter, and pack the wine in an insulated bag. Flavor some melted butter with lemon juice (about 1 teaspoon per ¼ pound of butter), place in a container, and pack in another insulated bag while still warm—you're ready to go.

Lord and Master Picnic

So named because you'd do this only for the man of the hour, but we both agree he'll be *your* slave when all is said and done.

HEAVENLY CORNISH HENS

SESAME BREAD

ROQUEFORT CHEESE   FRESH PEARS

CHILLED WHITE WINE

Heavenly Cornish Hens

2 fat little 1-pound Cornish hens
¼ teaspoon garlic powder♥

♥ Go on. Peel a couple of cloves of fresh garlic and mash them any old way you can—a doorstop or a hammer will do in a pinch. Told you to buy a press.

> *2 teaspoons thyme*
> *½ teaspoon salt*
> *½ teaspoon pepper*
> *⅓ cup butter*
> *½ cup butter, melted*
> *¼ cup lemon juice*
> *¼ teaspoon paprika*
> *1 fat pinch thyme*

Wipe out the cavities of the unsuspecting beasts and fill each one with ⅛ teaspoon garlic powder, 1 teaspoon thyme, ¼ teaspoon salt, and ¼ teaspoon pepper. Tie their hind ends together with those little skewer-string affairs to be found in your market. Tie the legs together and literally bend their arms behind their backs. Melt the ⅓ cup butter in a skillet and brown the hens all over. Place on the bottom of a shallow roasting pan. Muddle the remaining ingredients together lovingly. Brush the birds often with this sauce while they are roasting at 425° F. for 40 minutes. Remove from oven and let stand until cold.† Remove all trussings and pack in an insulated bag when you're ready to trip off to commune with Nature.

Sesame Bread

That fancy Sesame Bread is nothing but good old French bread buttered and heated with some toasted sesame seeds sprinkled generously atop.

El Matador's Picnic

BARBECUED STEAK
RAW TOMATO WEDGES
GUACAMOLE WITH GRAPEFRUIT
CHOCOLATE FUDGE CAKE

If you have a friend who is in a black depression because he can't make it to Pamplona for the running of the bulls next year, pack up a picnic hamper, slip in a copy of *Death in the Afternoon,* and make haste for the countryside. While ordinarily you will want to hog all the glory of your picnics, this is one occasion to share the honors. If your aficionado is like most, he will love to select and bring the steaks and then barbecue them tenderly once you have gotten to your Andalusian plain. He'll think you're wonderful for having suggested it, and you will have saved enough on groceries to buy a pair of castanets and a black lace mantilla.

Since you have so adroitly foisted the main dish off on poor Ricardo, you can take your time preparing the accompaniments. Make up a batch of guacamole,* pack in a plastic container, and sprinkle liberally with lemon juice before covering. Take along two chilled grapefruits, which you will peel and section on the spot for dunking. ¡*Ándale!*

Chocolate fudge cake may be a bit incongruous in this Spanish atmosphere, but if you whip up the gooiest one imaginable from a mix, he won't mind a bit and you will maintain your status as chief of the culinary world. This is an important point to remember, as men tend to be insufferably proud of any food that passes through their hairy hands.

A posh picnic is not only a marvelous vehicle for romance, for if you're courageous enough to make it a picnic for four or six or even eight, your guests are bound to think you're So Clever. And best of all, you won't have any crumbs on your carpet when the sun's over the yardarm.

9

Happiness Is a Very Dry Martini

. . . **A**t someone else's party. To our mind, the drive to *give* cocktail parties must come from the same place as the urge that makes some clamor to tiptoe across hot coals in their bare feet. Oh, yes, there are a few acceptable excuses for hostessing a cocktail party, like the fact that it's a good way to make a clean sweep of your social obligations. We found that these parties were a perfect opportunity to bring all our beaux together so that they could eye the competition and beef up their efforts on our behalf. Or perhaps you're one of those people who can't resist those arty cocktail party invitations and, once they are bought, find yourself sending them willy-nilly to friend and foe alike. Or maybe you just like to drink.

Whatever your excuse, you have really gotten yourself into a sticky wicket. As we have already made abundantly clear, we think that the giving of cocktail parties is an occupation best left to Washington hostesses and dashing young men-about-town. But, assuming that the deed is already done, we hope that this chapter will get you cheerfully through the evening with only minor scars on your psyche and your furniture.

First of all, may we suggest that the most important ingredient for a smashing party (in addition to an abundance of firewater) is your guest list. There is nothing that kills a party faster than little clumps of people leaning against a wall, drinking, and staring at each other blankly. To prevent this unsavory situation, we have learned never to assume that because people do the same thing they are naturally soul mates. A party of stockbrokers can be a pretty dull affair no matter how many fascinating tips they might be able to pass along. Vary your guest list and try to include as many different types and interests as you can. Otherwise you may end up with a gathering that more closely resembles an eighth-grade dancing-school party with all of the gentlemen on one side of the room discussing spark plugs and ski waxes and all of the ladies on the other side discussing why the men are being such boors. The main thing is to ask people *you* like—this sounds like a simple rule until you try to put it into practice.

We try to get our parties moving and our guests circulating by being at the door to greet each and every one. People arriving at a party usually feel nervous and unprotected, so it's up to you to take the situation in hand and introduce your newcomer into a group from which he can bounce off into others. This should get his blood stirring and lift your party from being just another round of free drinks.

The party itself can be as simple or as elaborate as you choose. Oftentimes the smaller the space, the warmer the party. A girl in our apartment house used to pack her tiny hutch with charming, attractive people, put on her gold-hoop earrings and turquoise toe ring, stack her record player with wild gypsy music, and serve gallons of premade martinis (starting with a whopper and declining in power throughout the evening).[?] Needless to say,

---

[?] Looking back, we're not sure exactly how we thought it is possible to defuse a martini—water it down? Anyway, the point is not to let your guests get legless at your party.

an invitation to one of these affairs was as valuable as two on the aisle for a Broadway hit.

When you send out those frightfully arty invitations that got you into all this trouble in the first place, remember to be perfectly clear about what your guests should expect. Cocktail parties often have a disarming way of becoming the Late Late Show unless the hostess keeps her wits about her.

If you are planning a 5–7 affair with only drinks and a few peanut-butter and seaweed appetizers, don't, for heaven's sake, send invitations that read "cocktail buffet," or your guests will come prepared to dive into a groaning board, and those wee canapés will be a dismal disappointment. Of course if you *are* planning a cocktail buffet, be sure to make that clear also—so that your guests won't make other plans for dinner, leaving you with six pounds of lasagna. Also, it makes good sense to emphasize the fact that you're serving food, since in most circles this will call for a return dinner invitation and can lead to all kinds of intriguing possibilities.

Now comes the central concern of the cocktail party— liquor—and how not to be caught short. This subject is rather disheartening because, as we all know, liquor is expensive and seems to evaporate at a party. A good rule of thumb, if you are serving mixed drinks, is to buy enough liquor for three drinks per person. This means that one fifth will take care of almost five guests. Then, when you've calculated your total, buy another fifth of each type of liquor you are serving for insurance.☉

We know that in some places BYOB (Bring Your Own Booze) parties are quite the thing. But we don't advocate them unless you are dismally poor and are having only very close friends. They don't do anything for your glamorous, independent career-girl image and should be relegated to your Fond Memories File—along with your stuffed panda bear and college pennant.

A better idea is to serve a big bowl of punch, which is far less expensive than mixed drinks and can be just as gay.

Fish House Punch

This one is traditional, and like most traditions, it got that way because it's so good.

1 quart brandy
1 quart peach brandy
1 pint rum (light)
2 cans (6 ounces each) frozen lemon juice

☉ These days you'd better also have on hand wine, beer, and bottled water. However, while tastes lightened up for a while, there now seems to be a swing back to the cocktail, although today's are as likely to contain mangoes, Cajun peppers, or blue vodka as they are gin, vermouth, and olives.

1 cup light corn syrup, then taste (add ½ cup more if you like it
  sweeter)
2 quarts plain sparkling water

Mix all the ingredients except the sparkling water well ahead
of time and let them blend for about 1 hour. Just before your
guests are expected, pour the mixture over a block of ice or ice
cubes in your punch bowl (or dishpan). Add the sparkling water
just before serving. *Makes 3 cups apiece for a party of 8.* If you are
having more, increase the recipe accordingly.

Fritz's Fun-Packed Monster Punch

This recipe, which may well be our country's secret weapon, was
revealed to us by its inventor, a former Senate page. If this is
what is served at Washington parties, it's a blessing that the
United States is still on the map.

5 bottles medium dry white wine
3 quarts white rum
1 quart dark rum
1 pint banana liquor (this may be hard to find, but persevere)
1 pound dark brown sugar
5 bananas, sliced
1 whole fresh pineapple, sliced
2 quarts ginger ale
2 quarts orange juice
1 pint pineapple or lemon sherbet

Mix all ingredients except the sherbet together and stand back. Now pour the mixture over the pineapple or lemon sherbet. Add another pint of sherbet each time the bowl is refilled. It's a good idea to have some pineapple or orange juice on hand to cut the drinks of those who feel they are too young to die. *This serves 30 people most generously (about 3–4 large cups apiece)* and can easily be cut in half for a smaller and less liquid party.

One of the most sensible reasons for serving punch is that you'll save the worry of who is going to play bartender. If you have decided to serve mixed drinks, then we suggest that you enlist the aid of one of your generous masculine friends. There is something terribly unfeminine about a girl sloshing around behind a bar, and besides, you'll miss out on all the fun. However, a gracious hostess will repay her stand-in bartender at a later date with a home-cooked dinner (see "Food Fit for a . . . " or "Deadly Little Dinners," depending on how deeply you've had to dig in the barrel for your swizzle-stick man).

Experienced cocktail party givers will tell you that there are some people who shouldn't even be allowed to sniff a cork—and you can be sure that at least one of them is on your guest list. Fortunately, some of these poor souls recognize their problem— so be grateful and have some tomato juice, ginger ale, or something nonalcoholic but inconspicuous for them.

If you do find yourself at 9 o'clock with a watery-eyed weeper or an overly amorous alcoholic, all you can do is quickly brew up some nice thick soup and some good strong coffee. In fact, that soup is a good idea in any event. A big tureen of cioppino* or minestrone,* along with French bread and fruit on the sideboard, will make your guests fat and happy and will prevent them from reeling onto the freeways with childish abandon.

Whether you serve that soup or not, you must provide your friends with some kind of solid food to cut the effect of your liquid refreshments and keep them from biting their fingernails. The following hors d'oeuvres⊕ are easy to make and yet show enough ingenuity to make those who serve sour-cream-and-onion-soup dip at their parties hang their heads in shame.

⊕ Hors D'oeuvres

Strictly speaking, an hors d'oeuvre is the first course of a sit-down dinner. We've always struggled to find an appropriate description for the bits and pieces that are passed around at cocktail parties. *Tidbits* sounds stingy and *snacks* brings to mind the sort of thing one mindlessly munches while watching *Desperate Housewives*. The best description we could come up with is *strolling food*. And so it shall be.

Idiot's Cheese Delights

½ *cup softened margarine*♥
2 cups shredded sharp cheddar cheese
½ *teaspoon Worcestershire sauce*
Dash Tabasco sauce
1 cup sifted flour

Toss everything but the flour into a bowl and stir it all up. Blend in the flour and squish it around with your hands. Form into a long smooth roll (about the size of the tubes inside paper towels).† Here's the beauty: you can either slice the roll into pieces about ¼ inch thick and bake them now at 350° F. for 12–15 minutes, or freeze the roll as is and bake whenever needed. Since we discovered this recipe, we've always kept a blob in the freezer, and our friends who drop in unexpectedly for a toddy are convinced that we are sleight-of-hand artists. *Serves 10.*

Hot Shrimp in Dill Sauce

2 pounds frozen shrimp,♥♥ *ready to cook*
¼ *cup butter or margarine*
½ *teaspoon salt*
¼ *teaspoon black pepper*

♥ We use butter for this now, but margarine does just fine in this recipe.

♥♥ We keep saying: fresh, fresh, fresh. This will put a crimp in your pedicure budget, but hey—you're worth it.

1 teaspoon dill weed
3 tablespoons lemon juice

Thaw your little shrimp and dry them. Melt butter in frying pan with salt, pepper, and dill. Sauté the shrimp in butter about 1 minute per side. Add lemon juice, cover, and cook for about 5 minutes or until you get bored. *Serve hot to 8–10.*

Clam Blobs

1 package (3 ounces) cream cheese, softened
1 can (7 ounces) minced clams
Dash Worcestershire sauce
Dash curry powder
Onion salt to taste
Garlic powder to taste
Toast rounds

Mix everything together but the toast rounds.† Pile mixture on toast and stick under broiler for 3–5 minutes. Sprinkle with paprika and serve now! Better triple this recipe. *Serves 10–12.*

Cheese Puffs

2 3-ounce packages cream cheese
1 egg
½ teaspoon grated onion

Beat cream cheese with egg until blended and smooth. Add onion and pile on rounds of bread that have been toasted on one side. Broil about 1 minute or until brown and puffy. *Serve hot to 10–12.*

Stuffed Mushroom Caps

1 pound whole mushroom caps
½ pound ground round
Salt and pepper to taste
Pinch dry mustard
Butter

Wash and destem mushrooms. Mix ground round with salt, pepper, and dry mustard. Stuff meat mixture into mushroom caps and dot with butter. Broil until bubbly. *Serves 10–12.*

Rumaki⊕

Chicken livers
Butter
Water chestnuts
Bacon

Sauté bite-size pieces of chicken livers gently in butter for a few minutes. Cut water chestnuts into 1-inch strips. Roll the

---

⊕ It makes us nostalgic just reading this recipe, for rumaki was *the* strolling food of the '60s. Everyone loved it then and thought it quite exotic. Guess what? It's still delicious. It must be time for a revival.

liver and 1 strip of water chestnut together in a thin strip of bacon. Fasten with a toothpick.† Broil bacon till crisp. Serve *hot.*

If you are lucky enough to have a chafing dish, you might serve Flawless Fondue* or perhaps:

Ferocious Franks

3 jars cocktail franks⸮
1½ bottles (14 ounces each) ketchup
¼ cup sugar
Liberal dashes red and black pepper
⅛ teaspoon salt
¼ lemon, seeded and diced fine
½ teaspoon ground cumin
1 teaspoon ground coriander
⅛ teaspoon paprika
⅛ teaspoon saffron
¼ teaspoon ginger

Mix all ingredients except the franks and simmer for 15 minutes. Plop either the small cocktail franks or regular ones sliced in 1-inch pieces into this sauce and let them wallow awhile until

---

⸮ We blush. In today's world of magnificent and imaginative sausages, look for precooked sausages and slice them in 1-inch slices on the diagonal. Grill them on your ridged grill pan for a few minutes. Then plop them in the sauce, turn, and face the crowd.

warm. Provide guests with long Japanese skewers or toothpicks for spearing. *Serves 12–16.*

These hot hors d'oeuvres are not difficult, but if you don't feel up to tackling them, you'll find some wonderful frozen canapés in your local supermarket. They just require a brief visit to the oven and a pretty platter on which to recline. But do serve at least one hot hors d'oeuvre—your guests will think you care enough.

As for cold tidbits, there must be millions—there are even entire books written on the subject. But we suspect that they aren't selling too well since so many hostesses discover one appetizer and stick to it with the tenacity of a bulldog. Try some of these and your head will swell with compliments.

Sardines and Cream Cheese

2 cans small Norway sardines
1 package (8 ounces) cream cheese
3 tablespoons chopped onion (use instant)♥
½ teaspoon savory salt
1 tablespoon Worcestershire sauce
Dash Tabasco sauce

♥ Well, actually, we wouldn't now—use instant onions, that is. But at least we should have reminded you to reconstitute the dried ones in a little water for a couple of minutes. Forgive us.

1 tablespoon lemon juice
¼ cup chopped parsley

Pitch the sardines into a bowl with the cream cheese and mash with vengeance. Add all the rest and chill for 3–4 hours.†
Spread on those asbestos-like crackers or use as a dip. *Serves 10.*

Mushrooms in Sour Cream

2 pounds fresh large mushrooms
Butter
1½ pints sour cream

Wash and dry mushrooms. Trim off about half of the woody stem. Sauté in butter until golden brown and serve, cap side down, on a bed of sour cream (better supply toothpicks for stabbing unless you don't care much about your carpet). *Serves 12.*

Marinated Mushrooms

⅓ cup wine vinegar
⅔ cup olive oil (or salad oil)
1 tablespoon chopped parsley
½ teaspoon salt
½ teaspoon pepper
½ teaspoon sugar
1 tablespoon lemon juice
1 clove garlic
2 pounds small fresh mushrooms, washed

Combine vinegar, oil, parsley, salt, pepper, sugar, and lemon juice in a huge old Mason jar or anything that has a cover. Add garlic clove (still intact) and mushrooms. Cover and marinate several days or hours in the refrigerator. Remove garlic and serve. This one is great for a party because you can make it on Wednesday or Thursday night and forget about it until zero hour. *Serves 12.*

Cheese Ball

½ cup cheddar cheese
½ cup Roquefort or blue cheese
½ cup cream cheese
1 tablespoon butter
½ teaspoon Worcestershire sauce or 1 tablespoon brandy
½ cup chopped walnuts
½ teaspoon paprika
Few grains cayenne
½ cup chopped parsley

Soften and blend the three cheeses; add the butter, Worcestershire or brandy, walnuts, paprika, and cayenne and shape into a large ball. Roll in parsley and chill.† Serve surrounded by a variety of crackers. *Serves 10–12.*

Vegetable Cut-Ups

In these days when everyone is being lively and thinking thin, your guests might appreciate a platter of garden vegetables instead of a calorie-laden selection of goodies. Try a pretty plate of radish roses, cauliflower florets, green pepper strips, and carrot curls surrounding a bowl of sour cream flavored with curry, garlic powder, black pepper, and dried herbs for dunking purposes.

If you have noticed a reluctance on our part to include those old party standbys—dips—it is because they are messy and usually inordinately tasteless. But there is one that stands bright and shining above all others.

Guacamole♥

2–3 avocados, mashed
Salt and pepper
1 large hot green chili, diced (chilis come in 4-ounce cans)
Onion salt
Garlic salt
Chopped pimento
Bottled hot pepper sauce

Mix all ingredients but bottled hot sauce. Then start tasting. Add hot pepper sauce a drop at a time and let stand at least 10 minutes between additions so that the flavors will have a chance to mingle. You'll know you have enough pepper sauce when you begin to have a ringing sensation in your ears. If the guacamole is to stand for a while, add the juice of 1 lemon, cover, and refrigerate.† *Makes about 2 cups*, depending on the size of your avocados.

♥ Guacamole

This was our beginners' guacamole, the one we cut our cocktail party teeth on. We even made it in Macy's the day after New York's first big blackout. We were promoting this book's first incarnation, and New Yorkers looked askance at this green stuff we were serving, but because of the feeling of camaraderie after the blackout, the book signing and cooking demo became a party.

Today we've updated our guacamole a bit. We've deep-sixed the chopped pimento, garlic salt, and onion salt and added chopped tomatoes and onions. We keep it fresh and green with lime juice and love the addition of chopped cilantro. And even with the hot peppers, you'll want some salt and pepper to point up the flavors. The nice thing about guacamole is you can add and subtract ingredients depending on your taste and passion for hot peppers.

There you have it. Choose several hors d'oeuvres, but don't try to make too many or you may end up spending your party with your head under the broiler. Two cold and one hot would be quite sufficient for a small party of 8–10 people.

A few more words of advice: be sure to have plenty of ice cubes on hand. You can scour the neighborhood before the party or buy one of the big plastic bags full of cubes. Have lots of paper cocktail napkins placed strategically around for sloppy eaters. It is also a good idea to have a clean sponge ready for any accidental spills.

That isn't really hard at all, is it? Still in all, we suggest that the next time you see some of those marvelous cocktail party invitations, you beat a hasty retreat home—or at least invite us!

10
Big Bashes

And then there was the night that one of us announced shyly over Humbleburger Soup* that she thought it would be fun to have the entire PR department for cocktails and dinner. If it happens to you, your reaction will be no doubt something less than ecstatic until your roommate goes all big-eyed and trembly-lipped and confesses that she's already invited them because she was so sure you would think it was a great idea too. Sort of a bash, she'll explain in a weakening voice.

After you have extracted a promise of unlimited wardrobe privileges, you'll smile wanly and decide that the only way to face the music is to turn up the volume a bit. So invite half a dozen more people just for good measure.

You'll discover that good things don't always come in small packages. A bash is by far the easiest way in the world to entertain and in some ways can be the cheapest. We're not trying to tell you that twelve people consume less food and alcohol than do two—it's just that they will consume cheaper food and cheaper alcohol more cheerfully. With bashes, the bigger, the better. Somehow, a large group of people doesn't expect good food, good drink, or good china. You can offer them beer out of a keg, beans on a paper plate, and fruit out of a basket without turning a hair. Chances are they'll remember the evening a lot longer than the time you served them stuffed mushroom caps and veal with truffles à deux.

Secondly, bashes are easy. You have a roommate, and for probably the last time in your life you are going to have help. True, husbands must also be considered as a breed of roommates, but there the similarity ends. When it comes to entertaining, men are no help at all. The handiest man will cut his finger on the ice tray and naturally have to go in search of an adhesive bandage before he bleeds to death, for heaven's sake. The doorbell is ringing and there you are still sloshing around in the Stroganoff.

Finally, your menu will probably be simple. You're more inclined to whip up a huge pot of beans for a crowd than you are a dozen individual crabmeat casseroles. Consequently you can make everything in advance, leaving you plenty of time to lie around and eat bonbons on the day of the party.

Loathsome as the sharing of secrets may be, it's a gracious art, so we suggest that you take a look at our checklist and put it up at least a week ahead of time:

1. Tack up your menu, and stare at it long and hard. Do you have the right dishes with which to serve your repast? What kind of wine to serve, if any?

2. Gather your recipes together and check to make sure you have all the ingredients and all the right kinds of pans for cooking.

3. What kind of canapés?⊕ If they have to be broiled, will that interfere with what's heating in the oven for dinner?

4. Are you going to serve only one kind of liquor, or actually have cocktails? How's your liquor supply? Do you have olives? Soda and mix, etc.?

⊕ See historic update, p. 168.

5. If you're serving buffet style (is there any other way?), plan a road map of the buffet table, deciding which dish goes where. Go through the motions if you're not sure.

6. What about a centerpiece? If it's to be fruit or vegetables, put them on your grocery list.

7. Have you enough silverware? Need to borrow some?

8. Lots of ice? Know of a ready source if you should run out?

9. Some kind of music?

10. Bathroom neat with a fresh bar of soap and clean towels?

11. Coasters and napkins?

12. Check your menu again.

Now you can drop your wig off at the hairdresser's while you're preparing:🕐

🕐 This one stopped *us* cold. But believe it or not, there was a day when smart young women all had a variety of wigs, postiches, falls, and other coiffure augmentations. You didn't honestly think all that big hair in the '60s was real, did you?

COMELY LASAGNA
GARLIC BREAD   TOSSED GREEN SALAD
FRUIT OR SHERBET

Comely Lasagna

2 pounds ground round
2 cloves garlic, pressed
3 tablespoons salad oil *ℓ*
2 cans (8 ounces each) tomato sauce
2 cans (14 ounces each) solid-pack tomatoes
1½ teaspoons salt
¼ teaspoon pepper
½ teaspoon oregano
12 ounces lasagna noodles
1–1½ pounds ricotta cheese
1 cup Parmesan cheese, grated
1½–2 pounds mozzarella cheese, sliced thin

Sauté ground round and garlic in oil; add tomato sauce, tomatoes, salt, pepper, and oregano, and simmer for 5 minutes. Cook
noodles in boiling salted water for 15 minutes. Drain and rinse
with hot water. In a big buttered pan, arrange alternate layers of
noodles, thin spread of ricotta, tomato-meat sauce, mozzarella
slices, and Parmesan cheese, finishing with a layer of the meat

---

ℓ Olive oil, please!

sauce and the Parmesan. Bake at 375° F. for 12 minutes, cover, and refrigerate.† Before serving, reheat for 40–45 minutes at 350°. *Serves 8; doubles easily.*

Garlic Bread

We expound on garlic bread in chapter 4.

Tossed Green Salad

Try Antipasto Salad* or Green Salad Marinara.*

If you're poor and/or have an outdoor area of some kind, have a Bring Your Own Steak party. Each guest can barbecue his or her steak to desired doneness while you whip up the rest of the following menu:

BARBECUED STEAK
CHEESE-ONION MUFFINS
FOUR BEAN SALAD   BEER
GOOEY BAKED ALASKA

Barbecued Steak

Remember that succulent steak you had for the man's man in chapter 4? Why don't you try it again here?

Cheese-Onion Muffins

3 cups prepared biscuit mix
1¼ teaspoons onion salt
1 cup shredded cheddar cheese
1¼ cups milk
1 can (3½ ounces) french fried onions, crumbled

Combine biscuit mix, onion salt, cheese, and milk. Stir until dampened. Add onions.† Fill greased muffin tins ⅔ full. Bake at 400° F. for 15 minutes or until golden. *Makes 1 dozen.*

Four Bean Salad

1 can (14–16 ounces) green beans
1 can (14–16 ounces) wax beans
1 can (14–16 ounces) red kidney beans
1 can (14–16 ounces) garbanzo beans
½ cup chopped green pepper
½ cup chopped Bermuda onion
¾ cup sugar
⅔ cup wine vinegar
⅓ cup salad oil
1 teaspoon salt
1 teaspoon pepper

Drain all beans. Add chopped pepper and onion. Combine sugar, vinegar, oil, salt, and pepper to make dressing, and mix well. Mix dressing and beans together and refrigerate for 24 hours.† Drain excess liquid before serving. *Serves 8; doubles easily.*

Gooey Baked Alaska

This one's back in chapter 5.

Judy's aunt,⊕ who lives in Honolulu, has a fabulous chili recipe (figure that one out). Unfortunately, it's terribly involved, and we were sure she wouldn't mind if we simplified it a bit. Here's:

AUNTIE MAME'S CHILI

TOSSED GREEN SALAD   ONION BREAD

BEER

Auntie Mame's Chili

2 pounds ground round
2 tablespoons butter
2 green peppers, chopped
1–2 onions, sliced
2 14-ounce cans red kidney beans
1 can (28 ounces) solid-pack tomatoes

⊕ Auntie Mame has gone beyond the reef, but we still remember her moxie when we stir up a pot of this special chili.

2 tablespoons chili powder or more
Salt and pepper

Brown meat in butter; add peppers and onions, and simmer
until tender. Add beans, tomatoes, chili powder to taste, salt,
and pepper; simmer at least 30 minutes. Sprinkle with grated
cheddar cheese and sliced pitted black olives, if you like.†
Reheat, covered, at 350° F. for 35 minutes or until bubbling.
Serves 6; doubles easily.

Tossed Green Salad

Try Château Salad.*

Onion Bread

Instant minced onion♥
Butter
French rolls

Sauté onion in butter until tender but not brown. Split
French rolls in half, spread with butter mixture, and slip into
oven for last 15 minutes while the chili is heating.

♥ Come on . . . you can do it. Mince an onion. If you refrigerate it
first, you probably won't even shed a tear.

If you're really daring, why not try:

PROSPECTOR'S BEANS
SWEDISH CORN BREAD   TOSSED GREEN SALAD
BEER

Prospector's Beans

3–4 tomatoes
2–3 medium onions
3 cans (16 ounces each) red kidney beans
Worcestershire sauce to taste
¾ pound bacon (each strip cut in half)
½ cup grated cheddar cheese

Slice the tomatoes and onions. Butter a deep casserole and make several layers of beans, onions, and tomatoes. Sprinkle the layers with a little Worcestershire sauce. Be sure to end up with a layer of beans. Leaving the casserole uncovered, bake at 325° F. for 1½ hours. Top with half of the bacon strips and bake again for 1½ hours until the bacon is quite done. Gently push the bacon down into the beans and top with the remaining half of the bacon. Cook again for another hour. Sprinkle with the grated cheese, and slip into the oven for another 30–40 minutes until cheese is melted and bubbly. *Serves 6.*

Swedish Corn Bread

2 ounces (½ stick) butter
1 scant cup sugar
1 large egg or 2 small ones⊕
1 cup water
1 cup cornmeal
1 teaspoon baking powder (heaping)
1 cup flour
Pinch salt

Cream butter, sugar, and egg together. Add water, cornmeal, baking powder, flour, and salt, and bake at 400° F. for 20–25 minutes in a large, flat pan. *Serves 6–8.* (Your beans will keep warm on a burner while the corn bread is baking.)

Tossed Green Salad

A good tart green salad would be good here. Again, try Château Salad,* or use a dehydrated garlic-cheese dressing♥ on assorted greens.

⊕ Any contemporary chicken would be humiliated to lay a small egg. Moreover, they'd be out of a job in a thrice. Just use a regulation twenty-first-century egg.

♥ If you're in too much of a frenzy to make simple vinaigrette, there are many good bottled salad dressings in your market. Besides, we want to keep Paul Newman's charities solvent, and the bonus for you is a quick glance at old blue eyes on the label.

These are better barbecued, but a broiler will do if you're a have-not.

MAKE-YOUR-OWN SHISH KEBAB
SAFFRON RICE   TOSSED GREEN SALAD

Make-Your-Own Shish Kebab

3 pounds boneless lamb, cut in 1-inch squares
    (your butcher can do this for you)
20 large fresh mushrooms
20 canned small Dutch onions⊕
3 green peppers cut in 1-inch squares
Lemon marinade

In the afternoon, marinate the lamb in:

LEMON MARINADE:
½ cup olive oil
¼ cup lemon juice
1 teaspoon salt
1 teaspoon marjoram
½ teaspoon thyme

⊕ We know the Dutch produce great tulips and daffodils . . . but onions? We simply can't remember why we made this particular designation. At any rate, any partially cooked small onions with or without a visa will do nicely here.

½ teaspoon pepper
1 fat clove garlic, pressed
½ cup chopped onion
¼ cup chopped parsley or 2 tablespoons parsley flakes

Wash and destem mushrooms and arrange on a plate. Drain onions and arrange on another plate. Arrange green peppers on still another. Drain meat, reserving marinade, and place on another plate. Provide skewers and let your guests alternate meat and vegetables to their own liking. Barbecue and baste shish kebab with marinade as you turn the skewers. *Serves 6.*

Saffron Rice♥

Prepare precooked instant rice for 6 according to directions on package, and add a few grains of saffron to the boiling water just before throwing in the rice.

Tossed Green Salad

The simpler the better—perhaps lettuces with just the Classic Oil and Vinegar Dressing.*

♥ Ounce for ounce, saffron is a bit more expensive than a Ferrari. If you don't have time or the inclination to start from scratch, there are many flavored rice mixes out there waiting for you to add them to your pantry.

If you're a lover of Italian food, you might check the chapter "Pandora's Box," which closely resembles a week's menu for the cast of *The Sopranos*. This recipe is great for family reunions, football Sundays, your nephew's Cub Scout pack, or getting together with the girls. It's the most comforting of comfort foods.

MOCK RAVIOLI

TOSSED GREEN SALAD   GARLIC BREAD

CHIANTI

Mock Ravioli

MEAT SAUCE:

2 onions, chopped

1 clove garlic, pressed

3 tablespoons olive oil

2 pounds ground round

1 can (4 ounces) mushrooms♀

1 can (8 ounces) tomato sauce

1 can (3½ ounces) tomato paste

♀ We'd use the same amount of fresh mushrooms, sliced. Or use dried mushrooms reconstituted in a little warm water. Dried mushrooms have a deep, rich flavor and keep almost as long as a fruitcake in the cupboard.

1½ *cups water*♥
1½ *teaspoons mixed Italian herbs*
Salt and pepper
1 *pound farfalle, butterfly or bow-tie pasta, cooked*

Sauté onion and garlic in olive oil. Add meat and brown. Add mushrooms, tomato sauce, tomato paste, water, Italian herbs, salt, and pepper; simmer 2 hours. Mix the following ingredients in a large bowl:

SPINACH MIXTURE:
½ *cup olive oil*
½ *cup chopped parsley*
2 *packages frozen chopped spinach, cooked and drained*
1 *cup soft bread crumbs*
½ *cup grated cheddar cheese*
1 *clove garlic, pressed*
1 *teaspoon sage*
1 *teaspoon salt*
4 *eggs, beaten*

Grease large casserole or two small ones. Fill in consecutive layers of pasta, spinach mixture, and meat sauce, ending with meat sauce.† Cook at 350° F. for 30–40 minutes. *Serves 14–16.*

♥ Substitute an equal amount of Merlot, Cabernet, or Zinfandel for the water, and your version of this dish will be ready to star on any Italian menu.

Tossed Green Salad

3 heads romaine
1 head bronze lettuce♈
6 tomatoes, cut in wedges
½ pound raw mushrooms, sliced
1 jar (6 ounces) pickled string beans

Toss with:

LEMON-OIL DRESSING:
¾ cup oil
¼ cup lemon juice
½ teaspoon dry mustard
1 teaspoon garlic powder♈♈
Salt and pepper to taste

This is a crisp, tart salad that sets off any Italian food well and
serves 14–16 handily.

♈ This sounds like a head of lettuce that has been out in the sun too
long. The idea here is to have a mixture of lettuces, so just pick up
one of those handy bags of mixed lettuce at the supermarket, and
you're off and running.

♈♈ Okay, now's a good time to try out that new garlic peeler and garlic
press.

Or you might fashion a tablecloth of newspapers, provide mammoth napkins or bibs, and serve:

FRESH-CRACKED SHELLFISH
CRUSTY HERB BREAD*
TOSSED GREEN SALAD*
BEER

The fresh-cracked shellfish can be found lurking in your local fish market, and the Crusty Herb Bread♥ you'll find neatly classified in the index. If you're lucky enough to live in California, giant cracked crabs are out of this world—and they make their own centerpiece!

You see? Bashes are so easy to handle and simple to prepare ahead of time that when your guests arrive, you too can slip into something cool—like a nice dry martini. No need to be racing about sautéing and forcemeating (bet you never heard of that one) and generally raising your blood pressure. Better to sit down and raise a glass instead. Aaaaah.

♥ As you'll see if you turn back to this recipe, we recommend using butter and thyme. That's fine, but you can also try whatever herbs you like and in whatever combination pleases you.

11
The Witching Hour

A midnight supper, like a picnic, should never be a spur-of-the-moment affair. Nor must it be an all-out bit of bacchanalia, as the ingenue magazines would have you believe. You've seen those glorious six-page color spreads. You just know that that sleek-haired girl is humming "Clair de Lune" (in perfect pitch) as she sets her well-polished seventeenth-century French dining table ($950) with her well-polished sterling service for twelve ($600). She puts the finishing touches on a centerpiece ($25) and sets out her fine old Sheffield candelabra ($350) just as the merrymakers arrive. She starts them off with caviar on toast rounds ($15) to be followed by a sumptuous Crab Mornay that she managed to stir up somewhere in between Mr. Kenneth ($25) and the manicurist ($5).⊕

All this is a lovely picture and shows off that MacDougal tartan hostess skirt ($75)⊕⊕ to best advantage, but a glance at your own material possessions probably indicates that somehow this just isn't The Real You. True, it would be nice to be able to entertain like Shiny Hair, but it isn't the least bit necessary. A midnight supper is such a glamorous event unto itself that all you need do is load your apartment with candles to dim the glare

---

⊕ To update these prices to today's economy, apply an inflation factor of 600 percent (according to the Bureau of Labor Statistics Inflation Calculator) and then put a cold cloth on your head.

⊕⊕ This once-fashionable little piece showed a little more leg than the Civil War–era hoop skirt.

from your plastic dishes. It just naturally makes people feel ritzy to be a part of that gay Play-till-Four, Sleep-till-Noon crowd.

Midnight suppers also combine quite successfully with cocktail parties. We can't forget the first cocktail party we threw. It *was* flattering that everyone wanted to stay forever, but we didn't get rid of the last guest until the wee smalls—and we had to drag him out of the dumbwaiter. The midnight supper followed by steaming cups of coffee provides a neat solution to this predicament and a sobering little finis to your soirée.

A really sobering note: an invitation to a midnight supper means only one thing to many men—you are dessert! In the interests of your untarnished virtue, we have offered menus for four in order that your roommate and her date can be around to provide moral ballast.❓

Now you have all day and all night to cook. No matter what your menu is going to be, make sure it's a do-ahead meal so that all you have to do is give it a surreptitious shove into the oven when the time comes.

We have to let you in on a secret. A midnight supper isn't served at midnight at all. It's a bit much to ask your guests to wait until the witching hour to eat; your best bet would be to try to serve your little repast around 11 or so. The one hour makes a tremendous difference between a hunger-sharpened he-man and a snoring dullard.

❓ Well, now, weren't we the coy ones? We later learned that girls with tarnish-free reputations rarely have any fun at all.

One other thought about time: don't plan a supper to follow an outing that just might last later than 11. If you do, it is certain to run late and you'll spend the evening chewing your hangnails and thinking of the six quarts of cioppino growing old at home.

Lastly, don't forget that a midnight supper should be a gourmet's snack—not a full-course turkey dinner. Limit your menu to something hot, a salad, heaps of wine (for sweet dreams and medicinal purposes only, of course), and never, never dessert. After all, did the gods need more than ambrosia?♥

Our first menu is built around a fabulous fish stew straight from San Francisco's Fisherman's Wharf. We guarantee you'll eat until you're silly, but what a way to die. . . .

CIOPPINO

GREEN SALAD   CRUSTY GARLIC BREAD

CHILLED WHITE WINE

Cioppino

1 large clove garlic, pressed
1 tablespoon parsley flakes♥♥
1 tablespoon chopped celery

♥ Although an interesting selection of cheese and a few grapes would hardly be out of place here.

♥♥ Minced fresh parsley will make your soup a star.

1 tablespoon chopped green pepper
½ cup olive oil
3 cups solid-pack tomatoes and juice
1 can (8 ounces) tomato sauce
2 tablespoons salt
1 tablespoon paprika
⅔ cup dry sherry
Generous pinch basil
3 cups water, or dry white wine
1 pound medium fresh shrimp
4 lobster tails
1½ pounds crabmeat
1 pound halibut fillet, cubed

Sauté garlic, parsley, celery, and green pepper in olive oil until tender. Add tomatoes, tomato sauce, salt, paprika, sherry, and basil; cook slowly for 15 minutes. Add water or wine and cook slowly for 1 hour. If any of the seafood was precooked, set it aside to be added during last 20 minutes or so. Shellfish go in first and simmer for 5–10 minutes, then cubed halibut. Simmer for 10–15 more minutes. Now add any fish that was precooked.† Simmer 10 minutes. This can be made entirely ahead of time and simply reheated. *Serves 4* with leftovers for a midweek dinner.℗

℗ Unless you are feeding a couple of lumberjacks and a tackle for the 49ers, this recipe is more likely to serve 8 than 4.

Green Salad

Try tossing endive lettuce with shelled whole walnuts and Classic Oil and Vinegar Dressing.*

This next little gem is a sunny French cheese pie, filling and delicious. Unfortunately there is a little last-minute work involved, but it's well worth it.

QUICHE LORRAINE
ENORMOUS GREEN SALAD
DOMESTIC CHABLIS

Quiche Lorraine⊕

1 9-inch unbaked pastry shell
10 slices bacon, fried and crumbled
½ pound Swiss cheese, shredded
1 tablespoon flour
½ teaspoon salt
¼ teaspoon nutmeg
3 eggs, well beaten
1¾ cups milk

⊕ Contrary to recent mythology, we found that real men *do* eat quiche—even the ones who say something like "I'll have another slice of that quick pie."

In the afternoon, bake pastry shell at 450° F. for 7 minutes or until lightly brown. Sprinkle all but 2 tablespoons of the crumbled bacon on bottom of shell; distribute shredded cheese on top of bacon. Cover with Saran or waxed paper; do not refrigerate. When your guests arrive, combine flour, salt, nutmeg, eggs, and milk; pour over cheese and bacon. Sprinkle reserved bacon on top. Bake at 325° F. for 40 minutes. Let cool for 20–25 minutes. *Serves 4.*

Green Salad

Toss your favorite greens with a packaged garlic dressing.♥

The onion soup menu is a real tearjerker, so best do the whole operation early in the day; a midnight supper is not the occasion for an emotional outburst.

GOLDEN ONION SOUP

TOSSED GREEN SALAD   WHITE WINE

Golden Onion Soup

(Read it and weep)

3 tablespoons butter
2 cups onions, sliced thin
2 cans beef broth

♥ See note on page 189.

½ teaspoon Worcestershire sauce
Salt and pepper
4 large toast rounds
Grated Parmesan cheese

Melt butter over low beat in large saucepan; add onion. Cook 15 minutes or until golden brown. Add broth and two broth cans of water. Bring to a boil, then simmer about 20 minutes, stirring occasionally. Add Worcestershire and season with salt and pepper.† Serve in warmed bowls, topped with cheese-sprinkled toast rounds. *Makes about 1 quart or enough for 4 servings.*

Tossed Green Salad

Château Salad* again, or take a look at your Fat Cookbook—it may have a jillion interesting dressings.

These tempting little pancakes can be a miserable failure if you've never ventured into their tempting world, so we'd suggest a trial run on old Charlie or some other unsuspecting soul.

CHEESE BLINTZES
TOSSED GREEN SALAD   WHITE WINE

Cheese Blintzes

2 eggs
½ cup sifted flour

¾ cup water
1 tablespoon melted butter
Pinch salt

Beat eggs. Add flour alternately with water to the eggs, beating with rotary beater until smooth. Add butter and salt. Heat your 10-inch skillet and grease liberally. Pour batter into pan, making one large pancake at a time. Cook until underside is done and turn. When set, turn out on a paper towel. Cool slightly† and smear 2–3 tablespoons of cheese filling (see below) on each. Fold edges to center, envelope fashion. Fry in hot butter until golden on both sides. Serve with sour cream and strawberry or blueberry preserves or, if you're feeling reckless (and rich), sour cream and caviar. *Makes approximately 12 blintzes or 4 servings.*

FILLING:
1 pound cottage cheese
1 tablespoon sour cream
1 egg
2 tablespoons sugar
Dash each salt and cinnamon

Combine all and mix to spreading consistency.† We assume that if you're using caviar, you'll omit the sugar and cinnamon.

Tossed Green Salad

Toss greens and garlic-pickled string beans with a dehydrated cheese dressing.♀

No cookbook would be complete without a recipe titled Little Something-or-Other Casseroles. This is clearly due to the fact that the author or authoress has run out of ideas. You guessed it. . . .

LITTLE SHRIMP CASSEROLES
TOSSED GREEN SALAD*   WHITE WINE

Little Shrimp Casseroles

½ pound fresh mushrooms
4 tablespoons butter, divided
2 tablespoons flour
1¼ cups half-and-half
¼ cup sherry
1 teaspoon dry mustard
Salt and pepper
2 dozen fresh shrimp, peeled and deveined
Grated Parmesan cheese

♀ See note on page 189.

Sauté mushrooms in 2 tablespoons butter until golden brown. Melt the remaining butter and blend in the flour. Add the half-and-half slowly and cook until thickened. Add the sherry and dry mustard as well as salt and pepper to taste. Add the mushrooms and shrimp to the sauce and pour into four individual buttered casseroles or ramekins. Sprinkle the tops lavishly with grated Parmesan cheese and bake in a 325° F. oven for 10–15 minutes. *Serves 4.*

Midnight suppers are easy and lots of fun, but beware of a terrible fate. Use them too often and you'll find the cads are inviting you out just in hopes of another sumptuous—and free—meal. Now isn't that just like a man?

12
Glorious Gifts

Birthdays and holidays have a nasty way of cropping up when you least expect them—like when you have just blown your savings on a new pair of skis. And you can be sure that even when you're slaloming down the slopes, you'll be struggling with that nagging question of how to buy twenty Christmas presents with a bank account that couldn't finance a new lipstick.

Well, hop right back on that chair lift. This chapter is for you.

You may not believe it, but even the most sophisticated and blasé of your acquaintances will be struck dumb with gratitude if you politely hand him something that has been brewed and stirred and conjured up by your own loving hands. If you doubt our word, just remember that your mother is still using those ceramic salt and pepper shakers you made in the fourth grade. And mothers are not alone.

However, that something must be so ambrosial that you not only will have given a gift, but will have firmly established your reputation as a gourmet and a creative genius. That is why there is only one recipe for Christmas cookies included. Christmas cookies are made only by the lady in the apartment downstairs who knits afghan squares and sends boxes tied with old shoelaces to our troops overseas.

When it comes to wrapping your love offering, you can rely heavily on apothecary jars, baskets, brandy snifters, and such. If the object of your affection doesn't lose his head and throw them out with the trash, they can be used for other purposes. Clear plastic wrap is handy for keeping things fresh, and it looks good, too. Plastic bags that come on a roll are great for wrapping that "homemade" bread. Just be sure to keep your head out of the bag.

If you're really scratching, you can just use some old mayonnaise jar and dandify it with a little foil, felt, fabric, or brightly colored tissue paper. Old peanut-butter jars have a touchingly earnest quality that relatives find very appealing.

This first recipe may well put you out of circulation for some time, so we suggest that you make it early in the Yule season. We've never known anyone with enough self-control to make this without taking a small nip now and then.

Boozy Bourbon Balls

1 package (6 ounces) semisweet chocolate chips
½ cup sugar
3 tablespoons light corn syrup
½ cup bourbon
2 cups vanilla wafers, finely crushed (about 5 dozen)
1 cup finely chopped walnuts
Sugar

Melt chocolate in double boiler over hot, not boiling, water. Remove pan from heat and stir in sugar and corn syrup. Blend in bourbon. Combine crushed vanilla wafers and walnuts in bowl; add to chocolate mixture. Form into 1-inch balls and roll in sugar. Let ripen in a container covered with plastic wrap at least several days. Then wrap handsomely and present to your dearest lush friends. They'll never know what hit them. *Makes about 4½ dozen.*

Chablis Cheese

1 package (8 ounces) cream cheese
4 ounces Liederkranz cheese
½ teaspoon celery salt
½ cup Chablis
1 clove garlic

Make this at least a week ahead of time. Like European women, it isn't worth anything until it's been around awhile. Mash cream cheese until it is soft, and whip in about half as much Liederkranz as you have cream cheese. Season with a little celery salt, and beat in about 4 tablespoons of Chablis at a time until you have used up all the wine. Rub the inside of an earthenware container with a clove of garlic. Pack in the cheese mixture. Cover tightly and let stand at least a week before you give it to your favorite cheese connoisseur.

Bodacious Barbecue Sauce

2 cloves garlic, minced
1 onion, minced
1½ teaspoons dry mustard
1 tablespoon prepared horseradish
1½ cups water
¼ cup red wine vinegar
¼ cup sugar
2 teaspoons salt

1 tablespoon lemon juice
¼ cup olive oil
1 cup ketchup
3 tablespoons Worcestershire sauce
Tabasco sauce

Combine all ingredients except Tabasco in a saucepan and bring to a boil. Reduce heat and simmer gently, uncovered, for 45 minutes. Remove from heat and season to taste with Tabasco sauce. Place the barbecue sauce in the container of a blender and whirl until smooth. This can be stored for several days in the refrigerator in a tightly sealed jar (put this information on the label of your gift). *Makes about 3 cups* and can be used to baste ribs, beef, ham, or sausage.

Charitable Chutney

Remember when you paid a week's wages for that dab of chutney at the gourmet counter? Your destitute but curry-loving friends will never stop thanking you for this:

1 cup prunes
2 cups seedless raisins
2 cups cored, pared, chopped green apples
1 cup cored, pared, chopped slightly green pears
1 cup minced onion
1 small clove garlic, sliced thin
6 medium tomatoes, peeled and quartered

3 *cups brown sugar, packed*
1½ *teaspoons salt*
½ *cup chopped preserved ginger*
⅛ *teaspoon cayenne*

Cover the prunes with water and cook about 10 minutes. Drain, pit, and chop. Combine all of the other ingredients. Bring to the boiling point, then reduce heat and cook slowly about 3 hours. Pour into sterilized jars and seal at once. *Makes 3 pints.*

Pickled Mushrooms

1 *pint tarragon vinegar*
4–5 *cloves*
12 *peppercorns*
1 *tablespoon coarse salt*
1 *pound small mushrooms*
2 *tablespoons salad oil*

Simmer vinegar, cloves, peppercorns, and salt for about 10 minutes. Let cool. Wash the mushrooms, dry, and remove stems. Boil in salted water until just tender. Drain and let stand until cold. Pack loosely in jars. Cover with the cooled vinegar mixture. Add the oil. Seal with tight-fitting lid. Shake well. Let stand in cold place for several days. These have a sharp tang that's marvelous with cocktails. *Fills 4 6-ounce jars.*

Ye Olde Snack Mix

This is so simple that it's embarrassing, and it certainly will never impress a beau. But it will thrill old Charlie and will keep him from biting his fingernails while he ties those trout flies.

⅓ cup butter or margarine
¼ cup steak sauce
2 teaspoons seasoned salt
2 cups bite-size shredded rice cereal
2 cups bite-size shredded corn cereal
2 cups bite-size shredded wheat cereal
1 cup pretzel sticks
1 cup shelled nuts

Melt butter in a shallow pan over low heat. Stir in steak sauce and salt. Add cereals, pretzels, and nuts. Mix over low heat until all pieces are coated. Heat at 250° F. for 1 hour. Stir when you think of it. Spread out on absorbent paper to cool. Store in airtight container. *Makes 7 cups (6 if you've been snitching).*

Aristocratic Pâté

A treasure that even your haughtiest acquaintances will cherish.

PÂTÉ:
3 cans (4½ ounces) liver pâté
3 ounces cream cheese, softened

1 tablespoon grated onion
2 tablespoons finely chopped walnuts
2 tablespoons lemon juice

FROSTING:
4½ ounces cream cheese, softened
1 tablespoon milk
Pitted black olives, sliced
Pimento strips

In a bowl, mix the pâté with 3 ounces cream cheese, onion, walnuts, and lemon juice. Line a 3-cup bowl with waxed-paper strips, letting the strips hang out over the bowl. Pack pâté into the bowl, patting down firmly. Refrigerate, covered, for at least 3 hours. To prepare the frosting, beat 4½ ounces cream cheese and milk until the mixture is smooth and fluffy. Run a knife or spatula around the edge of the pâté and invert it on a plate (perhaps a good-looking paper plate if the pâté is to be a gift). Remove the waxed paper and frost the pâté with the cream cheese–milk mixture. Now take those olive and pimento slices and decorate the frosted pâté with flowers or whatever your artistic urges dictate.

Noëls

This is our single concession to the Christmas cookie set, but be assured that it bears not the slightest relationship to the cookies that the Lawrence Welk–loving⊕ lady downstairs whips up.

⅓ cup butter, softened
1 teaspoon vanilla extract
¾ cup light brown sugar
1 egg
1¼ cups sifted flour
½ teaspoon salt
¼ teaspoon baking powder
½ teaspoon baking soda
½ cup sour cream
36 pitted dates
36 walnut halves
Icing

Cream butter and vanilla; gradually beat in sugar. Add egg and beat well. Sift dry ingredients and add alternately with sour cream. Stuff dates with walnut halves and roll in dough. When well covered, drop from a fork onto well-greased cookie sheet. Bake at 400° F. about 10 minutes. When cold, spread with icing. *Makes about 3 dozen.*

⸻

⊕ Lawrence Welk was an antediluvian bandleader who, on his once popular television show, was backed by a gaggle of crinolined chanteuses and a hyperactive bubble machine. Don't ask. It was harmless.

Icing:

Melt 2 tablespoons butter; blend in 1 cup confectioners' sugar, 1 teaspoon vanilla, and 1 tablespoon cream.

If you have a friend who is defending our country on a far-distant shore, for heaven's sake, don't send him these. He'd wind up with a box full of crumbs. Besides, he'd much rather get the latest issue of *Playboy*.

Braggart's Homemade Bread

Scrounge around the frozen-food department of your local supermarket until you find a loaf of unbaked frozen bread. Take it home and read the directions. Then follow them. And seal your lips forever to the fact that you didn't grind the wheat yourself and bake it on your own humble hearth.

Now you can sit down and rest your feet with a satisfied sigh. And remember: there is no reason to feel one bit guilty when you rustle the tissue surrounding that mink hostess skirt from old BBD&O. When he opens his jar of Boozy Bourbon Balls, he'll feel like a piker. And, by the way, a word of advice: next year why don't you open a Christmas Club account?

Vital Statistics

It is boring little items like these that keep young girls out of the kitchen. There is certainly no need to waste any time trying to learn them; just remember they are here if you should need them.

3 teaspoons = 1 tablespoon
4 tablespoons = ¼ cup
16 tablespoons = 1 cup
1 cup = 8 ounces
2 cups = 1 pint
4 cups = 1 quart
4 quarts = 1 gallon

1 cup raw rice becomes about 3½ cups when cooked
Macaroni doubles itself when cooked
Noodles increase in volume by ⅓ when cooked

Epilogue

Although we had no desire to make this book an engagement or marriage manual, we can't guarantee that a man, wooed by your epicurean triumphs in these days of aluminum-flavored TV dinners, will not immediately fall to his knees and beg for your hand. As a matter of fact, we must confess that, honest girls though we are, we have not told you the entire truth. Along the way Jinx met a Gallant Gourmet (not Lester) who wooed her with laughter, long lunches, and a 1949 Bentley named Baby.

Not to be outdone, Judy waltzed down the aisle as the culmination of an office romance with a dashing young executive who has a golf handicap of three (in his dreams!). It was gratifying to learn that these coffee-break courtships occur in real life as well as in the slick magazines.

Our editor optimistically tells us that most best sellers have a happy ending. Now that we've provided ours, we can, with a clear conscience, go back to lolling in the California sun.

Epilogue Redux

Forty years is a long time on anyone's calendar. For us it's been a jam-packed four decades with marriage, children, pets, travel, breaking bread with friends, much joy, and only a few bumps along the way. It's been a great life so far, and we know yours will be, too.

Jinx married journalist and author Jeff Morgan thirty-five years ago, and for more than two decades they have been wiggling their toes in the sand on the island of Tortola in the British Virgin Islands, where they are the owners of the Sugar Mill Hotel. They have written several books together, including *The Sugar Mill Caribbean Cookbook*, and for many years they wrote a monthly column for *Bon Appétit* magazine. When she's not snorkeling off the beach just below her home, cooking up a batch of Caribbean lobsters, or writing about food or her travels around the world, Jinx can be found painting watercolors of her adopted island.

Judy changed Jack Perry's bachelor status soon after they met at IBM. In forty-three years of marriage, they're accountable for two sons and four grandchildren. Never still for long, they've traveled to exotic haunts from Machu Picchu to the Great Wall and lived in many versions of Paradise—Laguna Beach, Sun Valley, and Indian Wells. Judy has owned her own design firm for thirty years, edited innumerable manuscripts for friends and clients, and taught creative writing to dilatory high school students. Today, she patrols her gardens, keeping the lavender and rosemary ahead of the dandelions, pursues macrophotography, and can still feed you a fine meal at the drop of an apron.

———————

To learn more about *Saucepans and the Single Girl*
and Jinx Morgan and Judy Perry,
please visit: saucepansandthesinglegirl.com

INDEX